ISSUES THAT CONCERN YOU

Student Drug Testing

Other books in the Issues That Concern You series:

Drunk Driving
Gun Violence
Medical Marijuana
Obesity

ISSUES THAT CONCERN YOU

Student Drug Testing

Patty Jo Sawvel, *Book Editor*

Christine Nasso, *Publisher*
Elizabeth Des Chenes, *Managing Editor*

GREENHAVEN PRESS
An imprint of Thomson Gale, a part of The Thomson Corporation

THOMSON

GALE

Detroit • New York • San Francisco • San Diego • New Haven, Conn. • Waterville, Maine • London • Munich

LIBRARY OF CONGRESS CATALOGING-IN-PUBLICATION DATA
Student drug testing / Patty Jo Sawvel, book editor.
p. cm.— (Issues That Concern You)
Includes bibliographical references and index.
ISBN 0-7377-2424-2 (lib. : alk. paper)
1. Drug testing—United States. 2. Students—Drug use—United States. 3. Youth—Drug use—United States. I. Sawvel, Patty Jo, 1958– . II. Series: Issues That Concern You (San Diego, Calif.)
HV5823.5.U5S73 2007
371.7'84—dc22
2006043352

Printed in the United States of America

CONTENTS

Drugs are a major concern of teenagers today. In fact, for ten consecutive years, thousands of teens who participated in the National Survey of American Attitudes on Substance Abuse have said that drugs concern them more than social pressures, crime and violence, or academic pressure. When teens were asked what about drugs caused them the most concern, the majority of respondents said, "Drugs can ruin your life and cause harm." The second most common response was, "I feel pressure to use drugs."

Student drug testing has been promoted as a solution to both of these concerns. First, drug tests allow schools to identify teens who are using drugs. This creates the opportunity for early intervention and treatment, minimizing the risk of ruined lives. Second, drug testing mitigates pressure on students who do not want to use drugs by giving them a believable alibi—"I don't want to fail the drug test."

Currently, one in five schools uses some form of drug testing. These schools usually require drug testing of students engaged in voluntary activities, such as sports and clubs, and of students who choose to drive to school. Students provide urine, saliva, or hair samples, which are then tested for the presence of drugs. At some schools, every student participating in sports or extracurricular activities is tested once a year. At other schools, the students' names are pooled and random testing occurs throughout the school year. Each school is free to design and implement its own program within a set of general guidelines.

Opposition to Drug Testing

Some students believe that it is wrong to make participation in extracurricular activities contingent on student drug testing. For example, Lindsay Earls, an honor student at Tecumseh High School in Oklahoma in 1998, was required to take a drug test before she could participate in the marching band and the

Lindsay Earls stands on the steps of the Supreme Court in Washington, D.C., in 2002. Earls believed that student drug testing violated her constitutional rights.

academic team. Lindsay took the required urine test and passed it. However, she felt that the test was humiliating and accusatory and that it violated her Fourth Amendment right to be free from unreasonable searches and seizures.

Lindsay's parents challenged the policy in court with the help of the American Civil Liberties Union (ACLU), and the case eventually reached the U.S. Supreme Court. In 2002 the Court ruled against the Earls and expanded a 1995 ruling, which had allowed drug testing for athletes only. Now, all students in extracurricular activities can be tested. The Court based its decision on the need for schools to protect the safety of their students, both from health risks linked to drug use and from other students who may be using drugs.

While some students view student drug testing as a violation of their rights, others oppose it for different reasons. Some believe that drug testing is a waste of educational dollars, as tests cost between ten and thirty dollars per student. Others contend that student drug testing creates a negative, prisonlike school environment in which trust between teachers and students is undermined. In addition, critics argue, drug testing may hinder participation in extracurricular activities, which is a proven means of reducing drug risk. Finally, some claim that it is easy to cheat on a drug test—rendering it useless at its best and a means of emboldening drug-using students at its worst.

Support for Drug Testing

Many other teens support student drug testing. Students at many schools feel harassed and pressured to participate in an activity they do not believe in: illegal drug use. Many of these students view drug testing as a powerful tool to protect them and their friends from the lure of substance abuse. One such student is Larry Buchanan, a high school student in southwest Allen County in Indiana, where students convinced the district to begin drug testing in 2005. According to Buchanan, "I have talked to kids who have stopped doing these things on the weekend because they don't want to get caught. Obviously, you can't catch every kid, but if you can save at least one life, to me that's priceless."

Buchanan's quote suggests that drug-testing programs can deter some students from using drugs. Supporters also believe that student drug testing can identify casual drug users and help them to avoid the pitfalls of serious abuse and addition. As stated by Peter Provet, the president of a substance abuse treatment center in New York City, "While teen drug abuse may begin within a context of experimentation and peer pressure, those who go on to abuse with some regularity—presumably the target of this testing policy—do so to self-medicate difficult, if not painful, internal states and escape from pressing educational, social, and familial problems." For advocates, the promise of helping such students justifies the financial and personal costs that a student drug-testing program exacts.

Some argue that all public school students should be tested for drugs. These advocates point out that under current programs, only those who participate in extracurricular activities are tested. However, students who participate in such activities are less likely to use drugs than students who are not involved. Therefore, current programs do not target the students most likely to use drugs. As recently as 2004, a bill was introduced in Congress that would require all students to be tested except those whose parents decline.

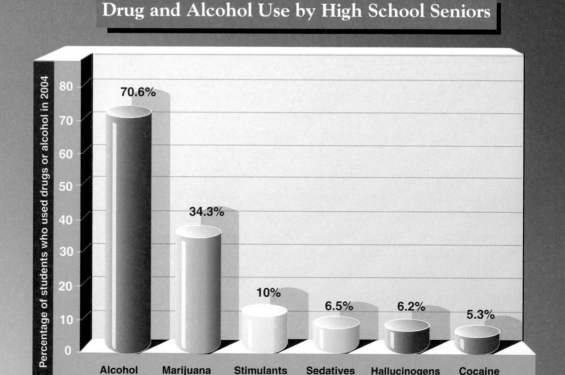

Drug and Alcohol Use by High School Seniors

Percentage of students who used drugs or alcohol in 2004

- Alcohol: 70.6%
- Marijuana: 34.3%
- Stimulants: 10%
- Sedatives: 6.5%
- Hallucinogens: 6.2%
- Cocaine: 5.3%

Source: U.S. Department of Justice, Bureau of Justice Statistics, "Drugs and Crime Facts," www.ojp.usdoj.gov.

Members of Students Against Destructive Decisions (SADD), an organization that favors drug testing, speak out against drug use at a Houston rally.

With drug testing present in so many schools—and potentially in all public schools in the future—this issue clearly affects all teens. In *Issues That Concern You: Student Drug Testing*, authors debate the effectiveness and fairness of such policies in excerpts from articles, books, reports, and other sources. In addition, the volume also includes resources for further investigation. The Organizations to Contact section gives students direct access to organizations that are leading the debate on student drug testing.

The bibliography highlights recent books and periodicals for more in-depth study, while the appendix "What You Should Know About Student Drug Testing" outlines the basic components of a standard student drug-testing program. Finally, the "What You Should Do About Student Drug Testing" section helps both supporters and opposers of student drug testing use their knowledge to help themselves and others. Taken together, these features make *Issues That Concern You: Student Drug Testing* a valuable resource for anyone researching this contentious issue.

ONE

Drug Testing:
An Overview

David G. Evans

The basis for student drug testing is founded in military, corporate, and government drug testing programs. In the following selection David G. Evans describes the evolution of drug testing in these institutions. In 1971, the military began drug testing soldiers returning from Vietnam. The early tests were fraught with problems, including false positives. After these problems were resolved, the military began conducting massive drug tests on new recruits and active military personnel. By 1984, drug testing had gained a significant foothold in corporate America. Nearly 30 percent of Fortune 500 companies used preemployment drug testing. However, little uniformity or regulation of drug testing programs existed. In 1986, the largest employer in the United States—the federal government—authorized drug testing of all federal employees. David G. Evans is a nationally known attorney who specializes in drug testing law. He is the author of several books about substance abuse and the law.

The use of drug tests began on a significant scale in 1971 on soldiers returning from Vietnam. A good history of the military drug testing policy is found in the case of *Williams v.*

David G. Evans, "Drug Test S 1:3 (Chapter 1. Overview of Drug and Alcohol Use and Testing)," *Drug Testing Law, Technology, and Practice*, November 2005, p. 1:3. Copyright © 1990, 2005 by Thomson West. All rights reserved. Reproduced by permission.

Secretary of Navy. Since 1981, the military has conducted massive drug testing on active duty personnel.

Random drug testing, where testing is unannounced and subjects have an equal chance of being selected, has been used, and it has been credited with a significant deterrent effect upon drug use by active duty personnel. For example, between 1981 and 1984, the rates of positive tests for Navy personnel under age 25 fell from 48% to below 5%.

Initially, the military had problems with false positives and other errors on drug tests. These problems were corrected by careful blind proficiency testing of the laboratories handling the tests and by improvement in the tests.

Government Begins Drug Testing

On September 15, 1986, President Reagan signed Executive Order 12564, establishing the goal of a Drug-Free Federal Workplace. The Executive Order made it a condition of employment for all federal employees to refrain from using illegal drugs on or off duty.

The Executive Order recognized that illegal drug use is seriously impairing a portion of the national work force, resulting in the loss of billions of dollars each year. The President reasoned that as the largest employer in the nation, the federal government had a compelling proprietary interest in establishing reasonable conditions of employment. Prohibiting employee drug use is one such condition. The Executive Order authorized drug tests of federal employees as well as opportunities for rehabilitation.

Pursuant to the Executive Order, the federal Office of Personnel Management (OPM) issued advisory guidelines for federal agencies in the form of the Federal Personnel Manual (FPM).

On July 11, 1987, Congress passed legislation effecting implementation of the Executive Order, in an attempt to establish uniformity among federal agencies' drug testing plans, to ensure reliable and accurate drug testing, employee access to drug testing records, confidentiality of drug test results, and centralized oversight of the federal government's drug testing program. The law, Section 503 of [Public Law] No. 100-71, mandated publication

by the federal Department of Health and Human Services (HHS) of guidelines in the *Federal Register* and that HHS certify all federal agency plans to ensure they follow HHS guidelines and the Executive Order.

HHS, pursuant to the Executive Order and the above federal law, issued mandatory scientific and technical guidelines for federal drug testing programs and standards for laboratories engaged in drug testing for the federal government in 1987, which were finalized on April 11, 1988. They have since been amended. Since then, various federal agencies have also published regulations on drug and alcohol testing that affect millions of employees across the country.

New military recruits line up for processing. All federal employees, including members of the armed forces, undergo random drug testing.

Corporations Use Drug Tests

In the private sector, by 1984, nearly 30% of the Fortune 500 companies were conducting preemployment drug testing. A study in 1987 found that of 249 large companies who participated in the survey, approximately 50% had a drug testing program. By 1988, a survey reported that 30% of companies with more than 5,000 employees reported that they used drug testing. Most large com-

A lab technician arranges blood samples used in drug tests. Most employers today require some form of drug testing of employees.

panies now have drug testing programs. The American Management Association in a 1997 survey demonstrated that 81% had drug testing programs, a 277% increase over the last 10 years. This has been helped by federal drug testing requirements such as drug testing of transportation workers. These studies indicate that drug testing has become pervasive throughout private employment.

In addition to the federal laws, many states have passed laws permitting drug and alcohol testing of employees, intoxicated drivers, and criminal offenders. . . .

Drug and alcohol testing are used to detect and deter substance abuse among law enforcement officers and other criminal justice employees.

To date, there is no evidence that the use of drug or alcohol testing is decreasing.

TWO

A Variety of Drug Tests: An Overview

Robert L. DuPont and Richard H. Bucher

Robert L. DuPont, is the founder and president of the Institute for Behavior and Health, a nonprofit organization that works to create new ideas for drug abuse prevention. He is the author of many books and articles on substance abuse. Richard H. Bucher, is the chairman of Drug Free Kids: America's Challenge, a nonprofit organization that provides family and community support for drug prevention. He is also director of the Institute for Behavior and Health and has worked with the White House Special Action Office for Drug Abuse Prevention. In the following excerpt DuPont and Bucher describe the various tests that are available to identify drugs in people. The most common drug test—and the easiest to cheat on—is the urine test. There are also hair, saliva, and sweat tests. All are designed to be painless and to minimize any imposition on the one being tested.

When people use drugs, including tobacco, the drugs also are found in all parts of the body. The drugs (and their breakdown products called metabolites) are excreted in the urine, laid down in the growing hair, and found in sweat and oral fluids (saliva).

Robert L. DuPont and Richard H. Bucher, *Guide to Responsible Family Drug and Alcohol Testing*, Institute for Behavior and Health, Inc., September 30, 2005. Reproduced by permission of the authors.

The most common drug test today is a urine test. Hair tests are also widely used and increasingly sweat patches and oral swabs are used to detect drug use. The chemical tests used for each type of sample are the same beginning with an immunoassay screening test and going to a more sophisticated confirming test, when needed.

Most workplace and school-based drug testing uses urine samples. Drugs are usually found in urine for 1 to 3 days after the most recent drug use. Marijuana can be detected for longer periods for people who smoke every day for weeks at a time but urine tests are usually negative after a day or two for people who smoke marijuana only occasionally.

A standard hair sample is one and a half inches long. Since hair grows about one half inch a month, this length of hair has information about drug use over the prior 90 days. Sweat is tested by

A drug counselor tests a urine sample for traces of drugs. This is the most common type of drug test performed.

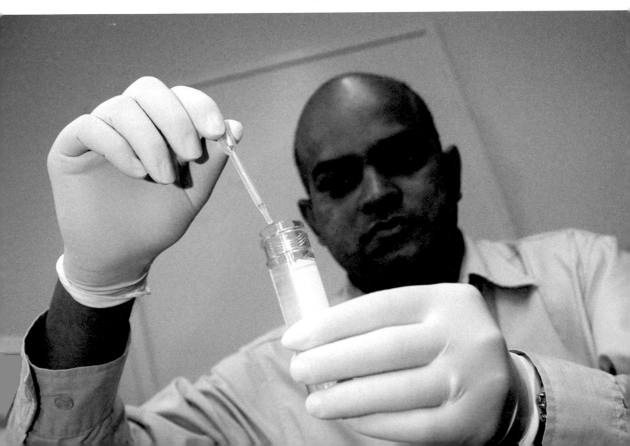

A Comparison of Home Testing Methods

Method	Normal Window of Detection	Ease of Collection	Limitations	Approximate Cost at Publication	Comments
Drug urine test	1–3 days since last use	Need privacy; awkwardness of urine collection	Vulnerable to cheating without observed collection	$12.00–$15.00 for 5 drugs	Additional drug assays (e.g., barbiturates, benzodiazepines) are available
Drug hair test	5–90 days since last use	Moderately easy; hard to cheat	Must be sent to laboratory; less sensitive to intermittent marijuana use	$60.00–$65.00 for 6 drugs	Includes Ecstasy
Drug oral fluids (saliva) test	Up to 2 days since last use	Very easy; hard to cheat	Less sensitive to all marijuana use	$16.00	

Source: Robert L. DuPont and Richard H. Bucher, *Guide to Responsible Family Drug and Alcohol Testing*, September 30, 2005.

applying a patch to the skin. Drug use is detected over the period the patch is worn, usually 1 to 3 weeks. Oral fluids are tested by taking a swab from a person's mouth. They generally detect drug use within the past day or two after the most recent drug use. . . .

Testing for Illegal Drugs

[The] urine [test] is the most widely available test and generally less expensive [than other types of tests] when testing for drugs of abuse. [Test kits] usually require that a small amount of the collected urine be placed in a reservoir and as the urine moves through the testing strips, results appear. But, urine has to be collected in a bathroom and is subject to cheating since drug users—including teenagers—are often clever at substituting someone else's urine or adulterating their samples unless the collection is directly and carefully observed.

Hair samples require that a small amount of hair be cut from the back and top of the head and sent to the laboratory. Hair samples give information about drug use over a longer period of time. However they are not as widely available and hair tests are substantially more expensive (about $60 per test compared to about $15 for a urine test). Hair tests will not identify drug use within the most recent 3–5 days, since that is the time it takes for new hair to appear that would contain the drug metabolite.

Hair samples are not only resistant to cheating, but the most widely available hair tests also test for Ecstasy, which is not tested for with most urine tests. However, hair tests are not sensitive to occasional marijuana use. In general it requires use about twice a week for 90 days to produce a positive hair test for marijuana. In contrast to their insensitivity to marijuana, hair tests are very sensitive to the other drugs tested and can detect them after a few uses over the course of the 90 days the typical hair sample covers.

Oral fluid ("saliva") testing requires a brief swab of the tested person's mouth. It requires no special training to take the swab and it is much less invasive than a urine test. It is also very difficult to cheat during an oral-fluid collection. However, the marijuana detection window is from ingestion to a maximum of 24 hours after drug use. On-site oral fluids tests, like hair tests, are relatively insensitive to marijuana use. Oral fluid drug tests for home use that provide an immediate screening result cost less than $20.00.

Sweat patches are not available to families now but may be in the future. They can be used by physicians. They are resistant to cheating and cover longer periods of time than urine tests (but not as long as hair).

THREE

Drug-Infected Schools Put Teens at Risk

Joseph A. Califano Jr.

> Joseph A. Califano Jr. has been chair and president of the National Center on Addiction and Substance Abuse at Columbia University (CASA) since 1992. From 1977 to 1979 he served as U.S. secretary of health, education, and welfare. In the following viewpoint he comments on the results of a national study. In 2005, CASA interviewed 1,000 students, aged twelve to seventeen, and 829 parents. The survey found that a student's risk for substance abuse is directly related to which school the student attends. Students who attend schools where drugs are used, kept, or sold are three times more likely to use an illegal drug than students who attend drug-free schools. In addition, schools with more than 1,500 students have higher rates of substance abuse, and public schools are less likely to be drug-free than private schools.

Our nation's schools are awash in illegal and prescription drugs. Since 2002, the proportion of middle schoolers who say there are drugs in their schools is up by a startling 47 percent, and the proportion of high schoolers attending schools with drugs is up by 41 percent.

Teens who attend schools where drugs are used, kept or sold are three times likelier to have tried marijuana, three times likelier to get drunk in a typical month, and twice as likely to have tried alcohol, compared to teens who attend drug-free schools.

We Are Failing
The practical meaning of these statistics is that this Summer and Fall, 62 percent of high schoolers—some 10.6 million—and 28 percent of middle schoolers—some 2.4 million—will go to schools where drugs are used, kept or sold. We are failing in our fiduciary responsibility to provide these children a drug-free educational environment and, in many cases, the result will be to deny them

High school students pass a joint around on school property. A student's risk for drug abuse is higher at schools where drugs are used.

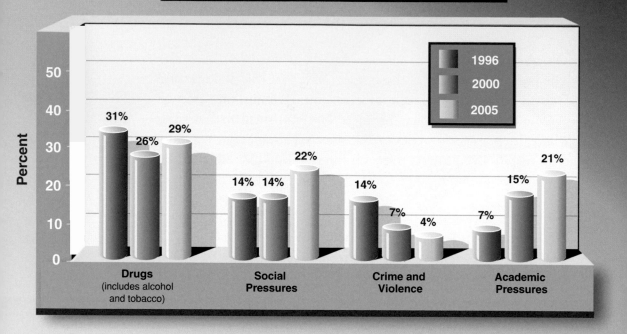

Drugs Are Teens' Number One Concern

Percent

Legend:
- 1996
- 2000
- 2005

Drugs (includes alcohol and tobacco): 31%, 26%, 29%

Social Pressures: 14%, 14%, 22%

Crime and Violence: 14%, 7%, 4%

Academic Pressures: 7%, 15%, 21%

Note: The survey was conducted by CASA and asked teens which of the following is their greatest concern: drugs (including alcohol and tobacco), social pressures, crime and violence, or academic pressures.

Source: CASA, *National Survey of American Attitudes on Substance Abuse X: Teens and Parents*, August 2005.

a drug-free childhood. These are the kids most likely to be left behind. It's time for parents to shout, "We're mad as hell and we're not going to take this anymore," and for education officials in Washington and the states, cities and counties to mount the same campaign to get drugs out of our schools as they are mounting to increase test scores.

The unfortunate fact is that so many parents accept drug-infected schools as an inevitable part of their children's lives. Forty-eight percent of surveyed parents said that drugs are used, kept or sold on the grounds of their teen's school, and an alarming 56 percent of these parents believe that the goal of making their child's school drug-free is unrealistic.

Increase in Peer Pressure

Another troubling finding from this year's survey—one consistent with the sharp rise in students attending drug-infected schools—is the increase in the number of teens reporting that their peers use illegal drugs. From 2004 to 2005:

- the percentage of teens who know a friend or classmate who has abused prescription drugs jumped 86 percent;

Mother and daughter share a heart-to-heart talk. Frank conversations between parents and teenagers can help combat drug use.

- the percentage of teens who know a friend or classmate who has used Ecstasy is up 28 percent; and
- the percentage of teens who know a friend or classmate who has used illegal drugs such as acid, cocaine, or heroin is up 20 percent.

Given the prevalence of substances throughout their lives—in their schools, among their friends—it is no wonder that teens continue to name drugs as their number one concern, as they have since we began conducting the survey in 1996: this year 29 percent of teens cite drugs as their top concern. . . .

- Most teens say legal restrictions have no effect on their decision to smoke cigarettes (58 percent) or drink alcohol (54 percent).
- Forty-eight percent of teens say illegality has no effect on their decision to use marijuana.
- Forty-six percent of teens say illegality has no effect on their decision to use LSD, cocaine or heroin.

Laws restricting teen smoking and drinking, and making illegal the use of drugs like marijuana and cocaine, play a significant role in combating substance abuse, but we must recognize that morality trumps illegality in deterring teen smoking, drinking and drug use. Parent Power is the most effective way to discourage teen drug use. Most kids get their sense of morality from their parents. In this survey, the message is and clear: Parents, you cannot outsource your role to law enforcement.

FOUR

Student Drug Testing Must Be Allowed

White House Office of National Drug Control Policy

The White House Office of National Drug Control Policy (ONDCP) was established by the Anti-Drug Abuse Act of 1988 to establish policies, priorities, and objectives for the drug control program of the United States. As a component of the Executive Office of the President, the ONDCP produces the report *National Drug Control Strategy*. In 2002, the Bush Administration issued its first *National Drug Control Strategy*. The strategy held the government accountable for reaching the following goals: (1) to lower the drug use rate by youth and adults by 10 percent in two years and (2) to lower that rate by 25 percent in five years. In February 2005, the president announced that the first goal was exceeded, as youth drug use declined by 11 percent. The five year goal is ahead of schedule. In the 2005 *National Drug Control Strategy*, excerpted here, the president set into action the most bold and controversial strategy to date—increasing drug testing of public school students. To support this initiative, the president's 2006 budget has earmarked $25.4 million for student drug testing programs.

Student drug testing programs . . . reinforce parental admonitions against drug use but also provide parents with needed information, even when the information is the good news of a

White House Office of National Drug Control Policy (ONDCP), "The President's National Drug Control Strategy," www.whitehousedrugpolicy.gov, February 2005.

negative test result. A campaign of public service advertisements sponsored by a public-private partnership confronts parental misconceptions head-on by equipping parents with proven techniques for monitoring teen behavior. Community-level prevention strategies include programs that support parents' wishes when parents

In a 2002 speech, National Drug Control Policy director John Walters urges parents to realize the importance of discussing drug use with their children.

cannot be there to watch, multiplying the number of watchful eyes in the community to deter young people from using illegal drugs or alcohol.

But all roads lead back to parents—and for good reason. Available research is unambiguous about the importance of having parents discuss the dangers of illegal drugs and underage drinking with their children. Parents and other caregivers need to do more than simply talk about drugs and alcohol. They also need to act—by monitoring the behavior of teen children, knowing where their teenagers are at all times, particularly after school, and knowing whom they are with and what they are doing. Such techniques have proved remarkably effective in keeping teenagers away from drugs.

Protecting the Adolescent Brain

Preventing drug use is important for many reasons—some obvious and some not so obvious—including recent scientific findings on the adolescent brain. Although the brain grows rapidly in early childhood, major changes are still taking place in the brain during adolescence. This is a time, according to recent research, when "pruning" of cells takes place. Certain cells live on and others die during this crucial time in brain development. Using substances that alter the brain while it is developing can have devastating long-term consequences.

In fact, the greatest single barrier to increased parental monitoring seems to be self-inflicted—the view of some parents, particularly baby boomers, that monitoring their child is nagging or, worse, authoritarian behavior that could drive a wedge between them and their child. Such parents may be more comfortable reaching out to their child as a friend rather than in the more customary role of guardian, monitor, and guide. They may struggle to reconcile their own past drug use, wondering whether it is hypocritical to lay down an unambiguous line that drug use is wrong and will not be tolerated. Worse still, kids report that parents are not typically as vigilant as their parents believe themselves to be.

Parental Monitoring Reduces Risks

The good news is that parental monitoring has been shown to be remarkably effective in reducing a range of risky behaviors among young people. Studies indicate that kids who are monitored are one-fourth as likely to use illegal drugs and one-half as likely to smoke cigarettes as kids who are not monitored. Put another way, the research confirms what many parents of teenagers tend to doubt: kids really do listen to their parents, and they do respond to parental expectations. For example, surveys show that two-thirds of youth ages 13 to 17 say losing their parents' respect is one of the main reasons they do not smoke marijuana or use other drugs.

The National Youth Anti-Drug Media Campaign, an integrated effort that combines advertising with public communications outreach, has drawn on these insights, in the process developing a series of advertisements that coach parents in monitoring teen behavior and promote early intervention against signs of early drug use. The President's fiscal year 2006 budget proposes $120 million for ONDCP's media campaign.

Fiscal Year 2006 Budget Highlights

- **Education—Student drug testing:** +$15.4 million. The President's fiscal year 2006 budget proposes $25.4 million for student drug testing programs. This initiative provides competitive grants to support schools in the design and implementation of programs to randomly screen selected students and to intervene with assessment, referral, and intervention for students whose test results indicate they have used illicit drugs. Funding of $2 million made available during the first two years of this initiative was used by 79 middle and high school administrators for drug testing programs. These efforts sent a message that local community leaders care enough to help those students showing warning signs of drug abuse and that they want to provide a drug-free learning environment to all students. With increased funding in fiscal year 2006, more schools will have access to this powerful tool. . . .

Student Drug Testing: The Saint Patrick High School Experience

Founded in 1861, St. Patrick High School is Chicago's oldest Catholic high school for boys. Five years ago, St. Patrick formed a task force of parents, community leaders, administrators, and faculty to explore the idea of a student drug testing program. The upshot was a recommendation to drug test all students randomly at least once each year.

"We have had amazing results from hair testing," says principal Joseph G. Schmidt. "We have 1,022 guys at St. Patrick. We have tested all of them, and only nine have tested positive. That's one percent."

Parents Pay for the Test

Each family with a child at St. Patrick pays $60 per year to administer the test, which can identify marijuana, cocaine, opiates, methamphetamine, phencyclidine (PCP), and MDMA (Ecstasy).

GAMBLE ©1996 THE FLORIDA TIMES-UNION KING FEATURES SYNDICATE

PARENTS

DRUGS

IF YOU DON'T FIGHT FOR HIM...THEN WHO WILL?

Ed Gamble. Copyright © 1996 by King Features Syndicate. Reproduced by permission.

In many schools, a positive drug test results in a referral to a counselor. Here, a student meets with a drug counselor.

A positive test triggers a notification of the student's family, at which point the student is typically referred to counseling. Consequences occur only if there is a second positive test any-time within a student's four-year high school career.

"First, they have a confidential meeting with me," says Rudy Presslak, dean of students. "And if it was a one-time thing and they feel they can stop on their own, that's the end of it. We encourage them to meet with the counselors here at the school, however, and if the parents feel that it's a bigger problem, they can see an outside counselor."

"We pull 10 to 15 kids [at a time] for hair testing," adds principal Schmidt. "It takes maybe five minutes per kid, mostly for paperwork. We snip an inch and a half of hair, which tells us if they have used drugs in the past 90 days. The parents are very supportive. And they appreciate getting the letter saying, 'Your kid tested negative.'"

The students seem to appreciate the program as well. "For the kids who would be tempted to use, it's an incentive not to," Schmidt says. "And for the kids who wouldn't use anyway, it's an easy way to say no when someone pressures them."

"The other day I heard a couple of our kids talking to a kid from another school," adds Dean Presslak. "They were telling him, 'We don't have drugs here at St. Patrick.'"

Student Drug Testing: Giving Kids an "Out"

Nearly three years have passed since the U.S. Supreme Court broadened the authority of public schools to drug test students, making this powerful tool available to any school battling a drug problem. Since that historic ruling, a number of schools across the country have seized this opportunity to implement drug testing programs of their own.

Student Drug Testing: The Polk County Experience

While shopping at a grocery store near her home in central Florida, Audrey Kelley-Fritz found all the proof she needed that her county's student drug testing program was working.

"I had a kid taking my groceries out to the car at the Publix," says Kelley-Fritz, who runs a student drug testing program for Polk County high school students.

"He said he didn't have anything to worry about with the school's new drug testing policy, but he was after two of his friends, saying, 'I keep telling them they have to give it up before school starts, because they [school officials] are going to find out.'"

Testing Creates Positive Peer Pressure

"Now that is what I like to hear," says Kelley-Fritz. "Not only are we making it easier for the one kid to say no in a party situation— this kid is exerting positive peer pressure on his teammates."

Polk County's program was begun after school officials decided to think creatively about bringing down the school district's drug use numbers, which are measured every other year by a state survey. "Our drug use numbers were higher than for the rest of the state," says Kelley-Fritz. "We were doing all sorts of things for prevention, but it just didn't seem like it was enough."

A community forum and federal demonstration grant later, the program was on its way. "Virtually none of the parents even raised a question about it," says Kelley-Fritz. "Most of the questions centered around why we were not testing for steroids, since we were testing athletes. Well, this year we are adding steroids."

A teen offers a joint to a classmate. Drug testing provides students with an excuse to avoid using drugs.

Testing Lowers Drug Use

Polk County had ample reason to believe that a student drug testing program would help drive down drug use. One of the county's high schools had started a testing program for student athletes in 1997 and saw marijuana use drop by 30 percent virtually overnight. The program was cancelled after four years because of a budget crunch, and drug use quickly returned to pre-testing levels.

Roughly 40 percent of student athletes in the county's 14 public high schools and a Catholic high school that piggybacked onto the program are tested randomly in a given year.

Athletes Are Role Models

"They sometimes feel that as athletes they are being singled out," says Kelley-Fritz.

"We tell them, 'You are the leaders of the campus. You have a responsibility.'"

If a student tests positive, the specimen is sent to another lab for confirmation. If the results are still positive, the specimen goes to the school board's medical review officer, who calls the parents and tries to account for any possible medical reason for the result. Barring that, the student is entered into a ten-day program of education and assessment, after which he can return to whatever sports activity he had been involved in before the drug test.

"From then on, they are tested at least once every other month, typically for a year," says Kelley-Fritz. "If they blow another test, they are removed from the team for the remainder of that season plus one calendar year."

Drug Testing Protects Students

Student drug testing programs are an excellent means of protecting kids from behavior that destroys bodies and minds, impedes academic performance, and creates barriers to success and happiness. Drug testing is powerful, safe, and effective, and it is available to any school, public or private, that understands the devastation of drug use and is determined to confront it. Many schools urgently need effective ways to reinforce their anti-drug efforts. Drug testing can help them.

Schools considering adding a testing program to their prevention efforts will find reassurance in knowing that drug testing can be done effectively and compassionately. The purpose of testing, after all, is not to punish students who use drugs but to prevent use in the first place. Testing helps to ensure that users get the help they need through a student assistance program, to stop placing themselves and their friends at risk. Random drug testing is not a substitute for all our other efforts to reduce drug use by young people, but it does make those efforts work better.

Indeed, student drug testing is that rare tool that makes all other prevention efforts more effective.

By giving students who do not want to use drugs an "out," testing reduces the impact of peer pressure. By giving students who are tempted by drugs a concrete reason not to use them, testing amplifies the force of prevention messages. And by identifying students who are using illegal drugs, testing supports parental monitoring and enables treatment specialists to direct early intervention techniques where they are needed.

As one high school principal put it, "For the kids who would be tempted to use, it's an incentive not to. And for the kids who wouldn't use anyway, it's an easy way to say no when someone pressures them."

FIVE

Student Drug Testing Should Not Be Allowed

Leah B. Rorvig

In the following selection Leah B. Rorvig rejects the argument that drug testing helps to keep students safe. As proof, she cites her experience at the boarding school she attended, which has a strict no-tolerance drug and alcohol policy. At the school, she reports, dorm rooms are regularly and randomly searched, surveillance cameras and administrators carefully monitor the premises, and curfews are strictly enforced. Despite these precautions, students abuse drugs and alcohol. Rorvig insists that the addition of drug testing would only add to the secretive atmosphere at the school. Such an atmosphere would be counterproductive, as research indicates that drug risk is lower when students have close relationships with their parents and adults at school. Instead of implementing drug testing, Rorvig argues, schools should work harder to facilitate connectedness and communication between students and the significant adults in their lives. Rorvig is the publications associate at the Drug Policy Alliance and a recent graduate of Columbia University. She cofounded the Columbia chapter of Students for Sensible Drug Policy.

As someone who just reached the legal drinking age nine months ago, I can tell you firsthand that a high level of surveillance doesn't make young people safer. And on the topic of student drug testing, the experts agree: Random testing does not effectively reduce drug use among young people.

The first large-scale national study on student drug testing, published last April [2003] by University of Michigan researchers, found that there was no correlation between a school's use of drug testing and the level of reported drug use among its students. That's why I'm surprised that President [George W.] Bush wants to offer $23 million to schools for drug testing.

At my high school—the Texas Academy of Mathematics and Science in Denton, one of the country's few public boarding schools—we were constantly under the purview of administrators and surveillance cameras. All 400 students followed strictly enforced curfews. We couldn't open our windows without approval, and the screens had stickers designed to reveal any escapes from our high-security dorm. Our rooms were searched randomly with bureaucratic regularity; students suspected of drinking were given Breathalyzer tests. One positive test result or an empty beer can was grounds for immediate expulsion.

Strict Does Not Mean Safe

You might think that we were the safest students in north Texas. But you'd be wrong. I knew classmates who drove drunk or high because they had no one to call who could pick them up in time to meet our strict curfew. Instead of opening up an honest dialogue, administrators enforced a strict no-tolerance policy, giving us the impression that we couldn't talk to them about alcohol or other drugs.

Thousands of students are subjected to drug-sniffing dogs, surveillance cameras in hallways and testing of their urine, hair or sweat. Some have to deal with even more traumatic measures. In November [2003], for example, 14 police officers stormed a South Carolina high school in a commando-style drug raid. After detaining and searching 107 students at gunpoint, the police found no

Hitch. *Liberal Opinion Week*, February 2, 1997. Reproduced by permission.

drugs. This search was based on the same "guilty-until-proved-innocent" logic by which we gradually surrender our constitutional rights for policies that don't actually make us safer.

Testing Receives Undeserved Credit

Now Bush wants to expand drug testing. In his recent State of the Union speech, Bush cited an 11% drop in drug use among high school students in the past two years, crediting student drug testing with a significant role in this decline. But the University of Michigan study, partially funded by the National Institute on Drug Abuse, found no difference in rates of drug use between schools that have drug-testing programs and those that do not. In fact, its authors found that 95% of schools do not test students randomly for drugs, making it unlikely that drug testing played a substantial role in the decrease Bush cited.

Drug testing without cause for suspicion has become more popular since a 2002 Supreme Court ruling upheld an Oklahoma school district's right to randomly test those students who wished to participate in competitive extracurricular activities.

For the past year and a half [since 2002], John Walters, director of the U.S. Office of National Drug Control Policy, along with the rapidly expanding drug-testing industry, has been busy promoting drug testing as the "silver bullet" to prevent drug use and keep kids safe. But such testing only would humiliate students and undermine their relationships with their teachers and coaches.

A police officer monitors the halls of a Texas high school for drugs. Some believe such tactics do little to deter students from drug use.

Open Communication Is a Better Choice

What really would make young people safer—and what kids sincerely want—are adults who will listen to them. A 1997 study by University of Minnesota researchers revealed that students are less likely to use drugs when they have close relationships with their parents and teachers.

Although I couldn't talk openly with my high school administrators, my father and I had a very trusting relationship. He was always there for me, whether I had questions about drugs or just needed a ride home from a party where there were no designated drivers. That bond made me much safer than any drug test would.

SIX

Educators Believe Drug Testing Does Not Work

Fatema Gunja, Alexandra Cox, Marsha Rosenbaum, and Judith Appel

In the following excerpt Fatema Gunja and her colleagues state that years of research and litigation have proven that random student drug testing does not reduce drug use among young people. Instead, the high cost of such testing diverts funds away from proven drug prevention programs. In addition, drug testing may actually increase the risk of harm by encouraging students to use drugs that are more dangerous but less likely to be detected in a drug test. Finally, because testing is limited to students involved in extracurricular activities, mandatory testing may inhibit students from participating in such activities, which are a proven means of reducing student drug use. Fatema Gunja is the director of the Drug Policy Forum of Massachusetts, an organization that seeks to reduce the harm caused by illegal drug use and current drug laws. Gunja has also served as the communications coordinator of the American Civil Liberties Union Drug Policy Litigation Project. Alexandra Cox, Marsha Rosenbaum, and Judith Appel are affiliated with the Drug Policy Alliance.

The first large-scale national study on student drug testing found no difference in rates of drug use between schools

Fatema Gunja, Alexandra Cox, Marsha Rosenbaum, and Judith Appel, *Making Sense of Student Drug Testing: Why Educators Are Saying No*. ACLU Drug Policy Litigation Project and the Drug Policy Alliance, January 2004, pp. 3–13, 16–17. Reproduced by permission.

that have drug testing programs and those that do not. Based on data collected between 1998 and 2001 from 76,000 students nationwide in 8th, 10th, and 12th grades, the study found that drug testing did not have an impact on illicit drug use among students, including athletes. Dr. Lloyd D. Johnston, an author of the study, directs *Monitoring the Future*, the leading survey by the federal government of trends in student drug use and attitudes about drugs. According to Dr. Johnston, "[The study] suggests that there really isn't an impact from drug testing as practiced . . . I don't think it brings about any constructive changes in their attitudes about drugs or their belief in the dangers associated with using them." Published in the April 2003 *Journal of School Health*, the study was conducted by researchers at the

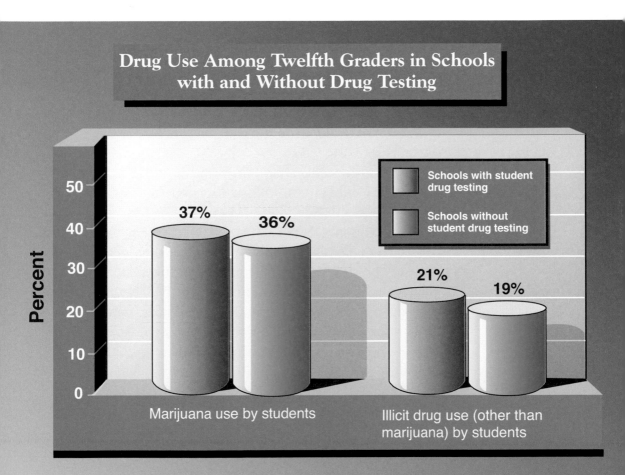

Drug Use Among Twelfth Graders in Schools with and Without Drug Testing

Source: University of Michigan Drug Testing Study, 2003; Fatema Gunja et al., *Making Sense of Student Drug Testing*, January 2004.

Studies show that extracurricular school activities such as band offer a practical way to prevent youth drug abuse.

University of Michigan and funded in part by the National Institute on Drug Abuse.

The strongest predictor of student drug use, the study's authors note, is students' attitudes toward drug use and their perceptions of peer use. The authors recommend policies that address "these key values, attitudes and perceptions" as effective alternatives to drug testing. The results of the national study are supported by numerous other surveys and studies that examine the effectiveness of different options for the prevention of student drug misuse.

Set against the evidence from this national study and expert opinion, a handful of schools claim anecdotally that drug testing has reduced drug use. The only formal study to claim a reduction in drug use was based on a snapshot of six schools and was suspended by the federal government for lack of sound methodology.

Who Says No to Random Drug Testing?

There has been a groundswell of opposition to random drug testing among school officials, experts, parents, and state legislatures.

Educators and School Officials

The majority of school officials—including administrators, teachers, coaches, school counselors and school board members—have chosen not to implement drug testing programs. They object to drug testing for a variety of reasons, including the cost of testing, the invasion of privacy, and even the unfair burden that student drug testing places on schools, with their concerns rooted in knowledge and experience about students. For many educators and school officials, drug testing simply fails to reflect the reality of what works to establish safe school environments.

Experts

Physicians, social workers, substance abuse treatment providers and child advocates agree that student drug testing cannot replace pragmatic drug prevention measures, such as after school activities. Many prominent national organizations representing these groups have come forward and opposed drug testing programs in court. These groups include the American Academy of Pediatrics, the National Education Association, the American Public Health Association, the National Association of Social Workers, and the National Council on Alcoholism and Drug Dependence. These experts stated: "Our experience—and a broad body of relevant research—convinces us that a policy of [random student drug testing] *cannot* work in the way it is hoped to and will, for many adolescents, interfere with more sound prevention and treatment processes."

Parents

Many parents oppose drug testing for the same reasons as school personnel and administrators. In addition, some parents believe that schools are misappropriating their roles when they initiate drug testing programs. They believe that it is the role of parents, not schools, to make decisions about their children's health.

State Governments

In 2003, several state legislatures have opposed student drug testing after hearing community and experts' concerns about privacy, confidentiality, potential liability, and overall effectiveness. For example, the Hawaii legislature tabled a bill that would establish a drug testing pilot program at several public high schools. In Louisiana, a bill that would have mandated drug testing state scholarship recipients was defeated.

Drug Testing Has a Negative Impact on the Classroom

Drug testing can undermine student-teacher relationships by pitting students against the teachers and coaches who test them, eroding trust, and leaving students ashamed and resentful.

As educators know, student-teacher trust helps create an atmosphere in which students can address their fears and concerns, both about drug use itself and the issues in their lives that can lead to drug use, including depression, anxiety, peer pressure, and unstable family lives. Trust is jeopardized if teachers act as confidants in some circumstances but as police in others.

Drug Testing Is Expensive and a Waste of School Resources

Drug testing costs schools an average of $42 per student tested, which amounts to $21,000 for a high school testing 500 students. This figure is for the initial test alone and does not include the costs of other routine components of drug testing, such as additional tests throughout the year or follow-up testing for positive results.

The cost of drug testing sometimes exceeds the total a school district spends on existing drug education, prevention, and counseling programs. In fact, drug testing may actually take scarce

A teacher comforts a student. Those opposed to school drug testing believe it erodes trust between students and teachers.

resources away from the health and treatment services necessary for students who are misusing drugs—seriously undermining the original purpose of the drug test.

The process for dealing with a positive test is usually long and involved; not only must a second test be done to rule out a false-positive result, but treatment referral and follow-up systems must be in place. In one school district, the cost of detecting only 11 students who tested positive amounted to $35,000.

Beyond the initial costs, there are long term operational and administrative costs associated with student drug testing, including:

- Monitoring students' urination to collect accurate samples;
- Documentation, bookkeeping, and compliance with confidentiality requirements; and
- Tort or other insurance to safeguard against potential lawsuits.

Random Drug Testing Is a Barrier to Joining Extracurricular Activities

Random drug testing is typically directed at students who want to participate in extracurricular activities, including athletics. However, drug testing policies may prevent students from engaging in these activities. Research shows the vastly disproportionate incidence of adolescent drug use and other dangerous behavior occurs during the unsupervised hours between the end of classes and parents' return home in the evening.

Research also shows that students who participate in extracurricular activities are:

Girls share a whiskey bottle at their prom. Some believe that random testing encourages students to engage in dangerous behavior such as binge drinking, which is less likely to be detected in a drug test.

- Less likely to develop substance abuse problems;
- Less likely to engage in other dangerous behavior such as violent crime; and
- More likely to stay in school, earn higher grades, and set—and achieve—more ambitious educational goals.

In addition, after school programs provide students who are experimenting with or misusing drugs productive activities and contact with a teacher, coach, or even a peer who can help them identify and address problematic drug use.

One of many school districts facing lawsuits regarding privacy concerns and confidentiality, the Tulia Independent School District has seen a dramatic reduction in student participation in extracurricular activities since implementing drug testing. One female student explains:

> I know lots of kids who don't want to get into sports and stuff because they don't want to get drug tested. That's one of the reasons I'm not into any [activity]. Cause . . . I'm on medication, so I would always test positive, and then they would have to ask me about my medication, and I would be embarrassed. And what if I'm on my period? I would be too embarrassed.

Drug Testing Has Unintended Consequences

Students may turn to more dangerous drugs or binge drinking.
Because marijuana is the most detectable drug, students may switch to drugs they think the test will not detect, like Ecstasy (MDMA) or inhalants. Knowing alcohol is less detectable, they may also engage in binge drinking, creating greater health and safety risks for students and the community as a whole.

Students can outsmart the drug test.
Students who fear being caught by a drug test may find ways to cheat the test, often by purchasing products on the Internet. A quick search on the Internet for "passing a drug test" yields over

8,000 hits, linking students to web sites selling drug-free replacement urine, herbal detoxifiers, hair follicle shampoo, and other products designed to beat the drug test. In addition, a new subculture of students might emerge that makes a mockery of the drug testing program. For example, in one school district in Louisiana, students who were facing a hair test shaved their heads and body hair.

Students learn that they are guilty until proven innocent. Students are taught that under the U.S. Constitution, people are presumed innocent until proven guilty and that they have a reasonable expectation of privacy. Random drug testing undermines both lessons; students are assumed guilty until they can produce a clean urine sample, with little regard given to students' privacy rights.

SEVEN

A Principal Says Drug Testing Works

Lisa Brady

Lisa Brady is the former principal of Hunterdon Central Regional High School in New Jersey and was a member of its Random Drug Testing Task Force, which developed one of the first random student drug testing policies in the United States. The student drug testing program at Hunterdon began in 1997 after it was discovered that more than 30 percent of its students in grades 10 to 12 had used marijuana. During the three years the drug testing program was operating, Brady argues, Hunterdon experienced a remarkable decrease in student drug use. However, in August 2000, the school was forced to suspend its drug testing program until the New Jersey Supreme Court ruled on its constitutionality. During the three-year suspension, the number of students who used multiple drugs increased 316 percent for ninth graders, 100 percent for tenth graders, 52 percent for eleventh graders, and 209 percent for twelfth graders. Following the July 2003 ruling in favor of Hunterdon, the drug testing program resumed.

Brady is the president of the Drug Free Schools Coalition and speaks nationally on the subject of random student drug testing. In addition, she has worked with the White House Office of National Drug Control Policy.

Lisa Brady, "Unlocking the Potential," *Student Assistance Journal*, vol. 15, Summer 2003. Reproduced by permission of the author.

This is how our program works: Each week, on Mondays and on one randomly chosen additional day, a total of seven students are selected through a computer program for testing. Their parents are contacted and informed that their child has been randomly selected for drug screening.

A vice-principal checks each student's schedule for the least disruptive time to bring the student to the health office for the screening. Our nurses read from a prepared script in order to ensure that everyone's experience is procedurally identical.

Saliva Is Tested

Since our switch from urinalysis to oral fluid collection for the random testing program, the entire process is completed in less than 10 minutes, including swabs for both illegal drugs and alcohol.

Each test costs $30, which includes the oral swab device. It also covers laboratory tests, including the initial and confirmatory test and review of the results by a medical review officer.

All of the tested students are athletes, involved in some type of extracurricular activity or in possession of a valid campus parking permit. In addition, about 5% of the 1,700 students in the testing pool have volunteered to be part of the program without being involved in any of the above activities. They, along with their parents, have previously signed consent forms agreeing to the testing as a requirement for participation.

The students are generally unconcerned about their selection but eager for the process to be completed.

Students Receive Counseling

At our school, students who test positive are temporarily removed from sports or extracurricular activities or have their parking permits temporarily revoked. They receive counseling and must attend four after-school drug education programs conducted by our student assistance counselors.

At Hunterdon Central, we employ the services of three full time student assistance counselors in addition to three guidance counselors at each grade level. These positions are funded by our

Board of Education. We have two youth-based services counselors who provide counseling in conjunction with our local medical center. These counselors work in the school but are not employed by it. Their salaries are provided by the State of New Jersey in conjunction with Hunterdon Medical Center.

We address the issues of alcohol and substance abuse through a strong, integrated curricular approach. In addition, we use a vigorous and aggressive approach to under-suspicion drug testing as mandated by New Jersey law and train all staff to identify and report any student who may be under the influence or need referral for substance abuse counseling services.

Students are not suspended as a result of a positive test, and nothing is put into their record. When a subsequent drug test

In 2002 principal Lisa Brady of Hunterdon Central Regional High School speaks on the importance of random drug testing in schools.

A counselor talks with a high school student. In many schools, students with positive drug test results receive counseling.

comes up negative, they can resume sports and activities and have their parking reinstated.

If a test is positive the second time, the same policy applies again. We've never had a third positive test, but if we did, it would be considered a more serious situation. We would still operate in a helping mode, however, and require more intensive intervention. Previously tested positive students also are subject to periodic testing which is not random.

Why Testing Began

As the principal of this large, suburban high school of 2,600 students, I have both administrated and implemented the random drug-testing program. I have witnessed the change in both the school climate as it relates to drug use and the positive impact it has had on the entire student population.

Our Board of Education, empowered by the US Supreme Court decision in the landmark case of *Vernonia School District v. Acton* in 1995, courageously acknowledged an alarming pattern of drug use among its students and instituted a policy requiring random drug testing for all students involved in athletics.

The board was prompted to take this aggressive approach armed with data collected in the spring of 1997 through administration of the American Drug and Alcohol Survey. It confirmed their worst fears. According to the survey, more than a third of Hunterdon Central students grades 10 to 12 had used marijuana, and more than 10% had used hallucinogens. In addition, 12% of sophomores had used stimulants, 12% of juniors also had used hallucinogens and 13% of seniors had used cocaine. The survey also revealed that a substantial portion of students perceived that illegal drugs were readily available, including 38% of seniors who reported that heroin was readily available. In a school of 2,600 students, the numbers added up to a lot of kids and a lot of drugs.

Testing Is Expanded

From September 1997 through August 2000, Hunterdon Central conducted a successful student random drug-testing program of students involved in athletics. Survey results from a follow-up administration of the American Drug and Alcohol Survey in the fall of 1999 indicated a remarkable decrease in drug use among the student population. Except for the introduction of the random drug-testing program, no other changes to the district's drug and alcohol program had occurred. A careful comparison of the 1997 and 1999 surveys demonstrated that drug use was down in 20 of the 28 categories. The survey also revealed, however, that use of alcohol, marijuana, cocaine and other drugs was still unacceptably high. In addition, parents, students and community members had made their opinions clear regarding the testing program being exclusively for athletes. They said an expansion of the program would be "more fair."

Based on a decision rendered by an Indiana court in the case of *Todd v. Rush County Schools* in 1998, the Board of Education voted to expand the policy in February 2000 to include students involved in extracurricular activities. The program now includes students involved in extracurricular activities as well as students who possess parking permits to drive and park on school property.

Hunterdon Goes to Court

In August 2000, the school became the target of a lawsuit filed by the American Civil Liberties Union (ACLU) on behalf of three students and their families who believed that the random drug testing policy was a violation of their Fourth Amendment right to [security against] suspicionless searches.

During the months that the case was being considered by a lower court in Somerset County, the school ceased the random testing program but began to experience a rapid increase in problems associated with school sponsored activities. For the first time in three years, students were found intoxicated on school overnight trips both in the United States and abroad. In addition, there was an alarming increase in the use of marijuana by student athletes as was reported by the student athletes themselves.

Although the school random drug testing policy was initially found to be unconstitutional at the lower court level, an appellate court upheld the case in July 2002, and our school re-implemented the program in December 2002. The case is currently being appealed by the ACLU to the New Jersey Supreme Court and oral arguments were heard in mid-February [2003]. . . .

The case involving Hunterdon Central is being closely watched by many school districts in New Jersey and nationally. They stand poised to consider random drug testing if Hunterdon Central is given a green light by the New Jersey Supreme Court. According to the National School Board Association, more than 750 schools are randomly testing and the numbers are increasing since the federal court ruling in June [2003].

Other Schools Benefit

In addition, two large studies, one in Indiana and one in Oregon, have posted positive results with students being randomly tested for drugs. A year-long pilot study of two Oregon high schools conducted at Oregon Health and Sciences University found that students subjected to random drug testing were four times less likely to use drugs than their non-tested peers. In the study, student athletes at Wahtonka High School were subjected to random drug testing while students at Warrenton High School were not tested. At the end of the year, of the 135 athletes randomly tested at Wahtonka, 5.3% said they were using illegal drugs. At Warrenton,

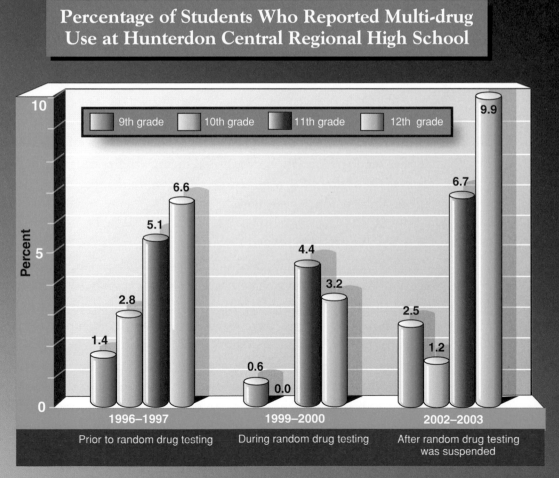

Percentage of Students Who Reported Multi-drug Use at Hunterdon Central Regional High School

9th grade   10th grade   11th grade   12th grade

1996–1997
1.4 2.8 5.1 6.6
Prior to random drug testing

1999–2000
0.6 0.0 4.4 3.2
During random drug testing

2002–2003
2.5 1.2 6.7 9.9
After random drug testing was suspended

Source: Student Drug-Testing Coalition, www.studentdrugtesting.org, 2004.

These teenagers seem unconcerned about drug testing. Schools that do not test for drugs report more drug and alcohol abuse among students.

19.4% of 141 athletes made this claim. In addition, student athletes at Wahtonka were three times less likely than their peers at Warrenton to say they used performance-enhancing substances.

In Indiana, principals were surveyed and asked to compare drug and alcohol activity during the 1999–2000 school year—when drug testing policies were in effect—with the 2000–2001 school year—when schools were not allowed to continue with their random drug testing policies. Eighty-five percent of high school principals reported an increase in either illegal drug or alcohol use among their students after the drug testing program was stopped.

Suspension Causes Backslide

At Hunterdon Central, over the three years that our program was suspended, student drug use among the highest risk category—multi-drug users—skyrocketed to increases of 316% for 9th graders, 100% for 10th graders, an increase of 52% for juniors and 209% for seniors. These results signaled a devastating backslide from the progress we had made during our three years of successful testing. In June 2002, the United States Supreme Court delivered its ruling in favor of student random drug testing. Upholding an Oklahoma school's drug-testing program that permitted the random testing of students involved in athletics and extracurricular activities, the federal court decided that the health and safety of schools and students outweighed an individual student's minimal privacy interest when it comes to drug testing. *Tecumseh, Oklahoma BOE v. Earls* hails a landmark victory for schools and communities who are using drug testing to protect all students against the dangers of drug use. Hunterdon is one of those schools, and we have the data to prove it works for us.

EIGHT

School Drug Testing Programs Are Flawed

Drug Detection Report

> The Guymon Public Schools district is located in Oklahoma. This small district has an annual K–12 enrollment of about twenty-four hundred students. In 2002, Guymon dropped its three-year-old student drug testing program because it found the program counterproductive. Not only were there few positive test results, but students were intent on cheating. Also, the random testing selection process was inconsistent: Some students were chosen for testing up to eight times in a given year, while other students were never chosen at all. Furthermore, participation in extracurricular activities declined while the drug testing program was in effect.

Amid the slew of schools that have decided to implement drug-testing programs following the U.S. Supreme Court decision, one school district, Guymon Public Schools, in Oklahoma, however, has determined to stop its three-year-old program.

"We didn't feel like we were getting our money's worth," Scot Dahl, vice president of the school board, told DDR [*Drug Detection Report*]. "Whether it was a deterrent [to drug use], we don't know."

The program, which cost from about $9,000 to $15,000 per year, was used in part to drug test bus drivers, who will continue to be tested.

Students Know How to Cheat

Dahl said the administration was continually finding out that students were defrauding the drug tests. They had balloons of "clean" urine, for example, they would tape to the inside of their legs.

Dahl said one mother called him saying her child actually drank bleach, having been told that was a way to beat the tests.

Another student, a football player, was randomly picked to take the test. And since he had smoked marijuana over the weekend he told the coach that he was going to have to quit the team. But the test came back negative, Dahl said.

Steve Kelley. Copyright © 1989 by San Diego Union Copley News Service. Reproduced by permission of the artist.

Girls at soccer practice listen to their coach. Teens participating in after-school activities are less likely to use drugs.

That type of scenario happened more than once, he added.

Furthermore, the drug testing company would send a list of randomly selected students to be tested about once a week. Sometimes one student would be chosen for testing six or eight times a year while another student would never be picked.

Extracurricular Activities Suffer

Dahl added that participation in extracurricular activities has been down. It is better for a student to be in an extracurricular activity, which is supervised, and not drug tested, than to be at home without supervision during after school hours. Studies have shown that the highest juvenile crime rate occurs from 3:30 p.m. to 8 p.m.

Students to Police Themselves

The board decided to try another route in deterring drug use, one that would cover all students instead of just athletes or students participating in extracurricular activities.

The school district plans to hire a liaison police officer who is trained to detect drugs. The officer will monitor the school and occasionally bring in drug detecting dogs.

The district also will implement a student crime stoppers program, Dahl said. A student will be able to call a number anonymously and tell the name of another student who is doing drugs.

Also to be set up is a teen court, which will take place at the county courthouse and have a student judge and jury. Sentences will involve community service work.

Dahl said he was told when studying two other school districts for ideas—Amarillo Independent School District in Texas and Jefferson County (which is the home to Columbine) in Colorado—that students who police their own schools "do a better job of it than adults."

The new programs will actually cost more than the drug-testing program because of the price of the police officer. . . . Nonetheless, cost is not the issue; it is whether the program is working.

Dahl said the school administration will evaluate the new programs after a couple of years and decide if they work better.

NINE

Student Drug Testing Is Challenged in the Courts

Adam T. Wolfe

In the following excerpt Adam T. Wolfe discusses the legal status of student drug testing. In a 1995 lawsuit, *Vernonia School District v. Acton*, the U.S. Supreme Court found that drug testing public school athletes is reasonable under the Fourth Amendment. In 2002, in *Board of Education v. Earls*, the Supreme Court expanded its ruling to include students in all extracurricular activities. However, schools are not just subject to federal laws. They must also abide by state constitutions and laws. Some state constitutions may afford students a higher level of privacy rights than those granted by the Fourth Amendment of the U.S. Constitution. This was a key issue in 2003, in *Theodore v. Delaware Valley School District*. The Pennsylvania Supreme Court ruled that student drug testing violated the Pennsylvania constitution because the school was unable to show a specific need for the drug testing policy. In other words, though the drug testing program was within the guidelines issued by the U.S. Supreme Court, it did not meet the requirements of the state. Similar challenges have been brought to court in Indiana, New Jersey, Oregon, and Washington. In each case, the state court upheld the drug testing policy. Wolfe is a 2005 graduate of Widener University School of Law.

Adam T. Wolfe, "*Theodore v. Delaware Valley School District:* School Drug Testing and Its Limitations Under the Pennsylvania Constitution," *Widener Law Journal*, vol. 14, 2005. Copyright © 2005 by Widener University School of Law. Reproduced by permission of the author.

In 1998, the Delaware Valley School District ("District") adopted Policy 227 which required "all middle and high school students seeking to participate in extracurricular activities or requesting permission to drive to school or park at school to sign, or have a parent sign, a 'contract' consenting to testing for alcohol and controlled substances." In addition to the contract, students involved in these activities ("target group") were provided a copy of the policy and its purposes. The statement of purpose indicated that Policy 227 was designed to effectuate the District's goal of maintaining a drug-free environment and prevent the consequences of teenage drug use. Furthermore, the statement detailed the District's reasons for selecting the targeted group of students, including their status as role models to other students, the responsibility of representing the school to the public and, most importantly, the inherent risk that comes with combining substance use and driving or participating in an athletic event. The Policy's target group not only included athletes and those seeking permission to drive to and park at school, but extended to all extracurricular activities, including the National Honor Society, Science Olympiad, Academic Bowl, and other similar clubs and organizations sponsored by the District.

Five Reasons to Test

Under Policy 227, students in the target group would be subject to testing under five different circumstances. An initial testing would be required in order for the student to be permitted to take part in an activity or obtain permission to park at the school. During participation in the activity, a student would be subject to random drug testing. This testing would be conducted monthly on five percent of the target group. The process of selecting students was based on a scientifically valid method that allowed for an equal chance of choosing each student. A student in the target group could also be subject to testing if an "authorized adult" formed a reasonable individualized suspicion that the student was using alcohol or a controlled substance. If a student tested positive for one of the specifically listed substances, the student would be suspended from the activity and, in order to return, would be required to submit to a "return to activity" test. This would be accompanied by follow-up testing in accordance with recommendations from a substance abuse professional.

Policy 227 also provided for a detailed set of procedures required when a student tested positive for one of the listed substances. Upon each positive test, a medical review officer would investigate to determine if there were any other possible explanations for the result. The student and his or her parents were given an oppor-

A lab technician examines test results from a urine sample. Random drug testing in schools typically employs urine samples.

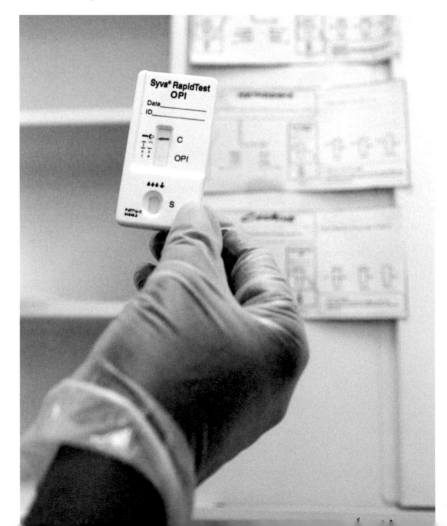

tunity to address the result, at which point, if no other explanation existed, the result would be reported to the school's principal and athletic director. The student or his or her parents could request a retest of the sample, but if they chose not to contest the result or if the retest was positive, the result would be reported to "need to know" personnel who are required to keep it confidential.

Students Are Disciplined

Once it was confirmed that the student tested positive for a listed substance, a parent conference would be held, and mandatory counseling would be assigned. The student would then be suspended from participation in the activity for a period of time and subject to weekly testing for six months. If a student tested positive a second time, the student would be suspended from the activity for one year. If it occurred a third time, the student would be prohibited from participating in the activity throughout the student's remaining school years. It is crucial to note that under the Policy, at no time would the test results be provided to law enforcement officials. In addition, a positive result could not be used by the school as grounds for suspension or expulsion and could not affect the student's academic standing whatsoever.

Facts of the Case

Kimberly and Jennifer Theodore, students at Delaware Valley High School, were subject to urine testing under Policy 227. Both girls were members of one of the groups targeted by the Policy. Kimberly participated in athletics and was permitted to park at school. Jennifer was a member of the National Honor Society and participated in the Science Olympiad and Scholastic Bowl. Each girl tested negative. However, the girls' parents filed suit, claiming that "Policy 227 deprive[d] students of their right to be free from unreasonable searches and seizures as guaranteed by [a]rticle I, [s]ection 8 of the Pennsylvania Constitution." Furthermore, they claimed a fundamental right in their ability to determine their children's medical treatment, and that this right was abridged by the imposition of mandatory counseling upon a positive result. . . .

Show a Specific Need

In *Theodore*, the Pennsylvania Supreme Court was faced with the issue of whether to require a public school district to show, upon implementing a suspicionless drug testing policy, a specific need in the district's schools and that a specific reason justified the targeting of a selected group of students. The court began by addressing the United States Supreme Court decisions that dealt with the Fourth Amendment and its application to school drug testing. In *Vernonia School District 47J v. Acton* [1995], the Court was presented with the issue of the constitutionality of drug testing student athletes. The school district was faced with a "sharp increase in drug use" throughout the 1980s, which was accompanied by increasing disciplinary problems. After unsuccessfully attempting less invasive measures to correct the problems, the district began to develop a drug testing policy, which was adopted after unanimous approval at a parent "input night." The policy only applied to those students involved in interscholastic athletics.

The Court held the policy valid and, in doing so, developed a test to address the issue of drug testing in public schools. The test was developed to provide a guideline for determining the reasonableness of suspicionless searches (drug tests in this case). Due to the special needs associated with maintaining a safe and productive learning environment, reasonableness is all that is required for school officials to search a student. In determining that the school district's drug testing policy was reasonable, the Court weighed three basic factors: "(1) the nature of the privacy interest at issue; (2) the character of the intrusion; and (3) the nature and immediacy of the governmental concern and the efficacy of the means employed to address the concern." In applying the policy to the newly developed test, the Court focused on specific evidence provided by the district in support of its position. This included the increasing drug and disciplinary problems within the district's schools, the inherent risk associated with combining athletics and substance use, and the documented fact that student athletes in the district were not only among the drug users, but were "leaders of the drug culture," via their status as "role model[s]."

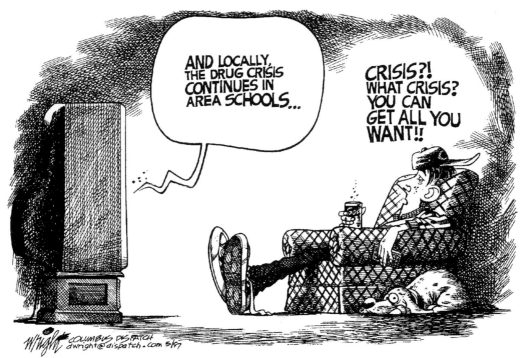

Dick Wright. Reproduced by permission.

Specific Evidence Is Needed

The *Vernonia* Court seemed to place significant weight on the specific evidence offered by the school district in establishing that a real drug problem existed and was largely a result of drug use by the target group (student athletes). However, there was no express statement indicating what specific evidence, if any, was needed to meet the requirements of the test and, in turn, the Fourth Amendment. Approximately seven years after the United States Supreme Court decided *Vernonia*, the Court shed light on the issue. In *Board of Education v. Earls* [2002], the Court upheld a policy which allowed for random suspicionless drug-testing of students involved in all extracurricular activities. The Court applied the *Vernonia* test, and in addressing the third prong—"the nature and immediacy of the governmental concern"—seemingly departed from *Vernonia*'s implication of a specific evidence requirement, finding that the Supreme Court "ha[d] not required a particularized or pervasive drug problem before allowing the government to conduct suspicionless drug testing." Furthermore, the Court reasoned that, "[g]iven the nationwide epidemic of drug use, and the evidence of increased drug use in Tecumseh schools it was entirely reasonable for the School District to enact this particular drug testing policy." The Court went on to reject the Tenth Circuit's dual reasoning that an "identifiable drug abuse problem" must be shown and it must be established that the members of the group subject to testing were major contributors to that problem.

Immediate Importance Can Take Precedence

The *Theodore* court found that *Earls* expressed the sentiment that due to the "pressing concern" of drug abuse in the nation's schools and impractibility of establishing a threshold of drug abuse necessary to hold the policy valid, there was no need to make a specific showing that a policy was necessary in the District. The *Theodore* court next turned its attention to the Pennsylvania decisions addressing the issue at bar. The court focused its attention on *In re F.B.* [1999 school weapons search case], which was decided in the interim period between *Vernonia* and *Earls*. The *In re F.B.* court established the Pennsylvania test, under article I, section 8 of the Pennsylvania Constitution, for determining the reasonableness of suspicionless searches in public schools. The test is based primarily on *Vernonia*, with no substantial difference except the language employed by the court. In contrast to the other cases discussed by the court, *In re F.B.* involved a weapons search and included the entire student body. The *Theodore* court found, however, that there was no reason the test articulated in *In re F.B.* should not apply to "searches which target a defined subset of the student population for after-the-fact evidence of drug or alcohol use." The court continued by addressing *In re F.B.*'s application of the test and explained the major points for upholding the District's use of hand-held and stationary metal detectors to search students for weapons. The reasoning behind the decision to uphold the policy was based on the minimal intrusion involved with metal detectors, the abundance of notice supplied to students and their parents, and the immediate importance of preventing weapons from entering the school. This immediate importance took precedence over any required showing of specific evidence of a particular need or history that may have been implicated by *Vernonia*.

The *Theodore* court furthered its examination of the specific evidence requirement by reviewing two other decisions that implied a specific showing was necessary. In addressing *Commonwealth v. Cass* [1998], a Supreme Court of Pennsylvania decision, the *Theodore* court focused its attention on the evidence of a "specific and increasing" drug problem in the school district. Furthermore, since the case involved a canine sniff of lockers before any search was undertaken, the court found that the intrusion on the student's

On the steps of the Supreme Court in 2002, Lindsay Earls (right) is confronted by a mother who lost her daughter to drugs.

privacy was minimal. Other important factors cited by the court in upholding the policy included sufficient notice provided to the students, a limited expectation of privacy in school lockers, and the absence of a specific target group.

Documentation Is Vital

The *Theodore* court also recognized the New Jersey Supreme Court decision on the issue at bar. In *Joye v. Hunterdon Central Regional High School Board of Education* [2003], the court held that New Jersey schools "will have to base their intended programs on a meticulously established record." This was evidenced in the case by the school district's showing of the two-year process which led to the adoption of a drug testing program similar to Policy 227. This included a survey of students, which indicated a high rate of

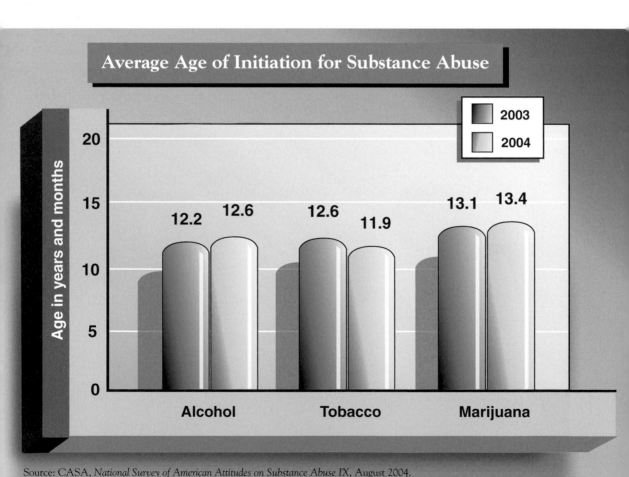

Average Age of Initiation for Substance Abuse

2003
2004

Age in years and months

20

15

12.2   12.6   12.6   11.9   13.1   13.4

10

5

0

Alcohol   Tobacco   Marijuana

Source: CASA, *National Survey of American Attitudes on Substance Abuse IX*, August 2004.

drug usage; the formation of a task force, which held hearings and conducted follow-up surveys; and an initial attempt by the school district to implement programs that were less invasive. Furthermore, statements were provided by school personnel that documented the increasing drug problem in the school district. In upholding the policy, the court warned that "a similar program at another school might not pass constitutional muster if, among other things, 'the underlying drug and alcohol use at the particular school is simply inadequate to justify it.'"

State Sovereignty Offers Great Protection

In considering the *Theodore* court's analysis of the issue, it is important to recognize the themes of new federalism that are intertwined throughout the court's decision. The notion of new federalism is based on the idea of state sovereignty and, in theory, allows state courts to grant greater personal rights under their state constitutions than are afforded by the United States Constitution. In a recent article, Justice Saylor of the Pennsylvania Supreme Court, stated that "'[n]ew judicial federalism' generally refers, more narrowly, to the increased tendency of state courts to interpret state charters as sources of rights independent of the Federal Constitution and interpretations of the United States Supreme Court." This notion of new federalism was evidenced in Pennsylvania by the decision in *Commonwealth v. Glass* , where the supreme court held, "The cases decided under [a]rticle I, [section] 8, have recognized a 'strong notion of privacy, which is greater than that of the Fourth Amendment.'" A similar sentiment was expressed in an earlier decision by the supreme court where it stated, "Article I, [s]ection 8 of the Pennsylvania Constitution . . . may be employed to guard *individual privacy* rights against unreasonable searches and seizures more zealously than the federal government does under the Constitution of the United States by serving as an independent source of supplemental rights."

In rejecting the "general problem" standard enunciated by the United States Supreme Court in *Earls*, the *Theodore* court relied on the themes of new federalism and, in particular, on its discussion in *In re F.B.* The *Theodore* court recognized that article I, section 8 of the Pennsylvania Constitution provided greater protection than its counterpart, the Fourth Amendment, and in doing so held that "a search policy will pass constitutional scrutiny only if the District makes some actual showing of the specific need for the policy and an explanation of its basis for believing that the policy would address that need." The court reasoned that since the *In re F.B.* test (the current Pennsylvania standard) is based on *Vernonia* and its implied requirement of a showing of specific evidence, it follows that this requirement must be met by school districts claiming validity of their drug testing policy.

Drug Testing Policy Failed Test

Keeping in mind the newly expressed standard that "a search policy will pass constitutional scrutiny only if the District makes some actual showing of the specific need for the policy and an explanation of its basis for believing that the policy would address that need," the *Theodore* court applied the *In re F.B.* test and concluded that Policy 227 did not meet the requirements of article I, section 8 [of the Pennsylvania Constitution]. The court summarily addressed the first two prongs of the test—the nature of the privacy interest at issue and the character of the intrusion—and indicated that the policy may be sufficient to satisfy these concerns. With respect to the first prong, the court found that students had a right to "reasonably anticipate" a heightened degree of privacy in their "excretory functions" that is greater than the entitled degree of privacy in their "lockers, clothing, or personal belongings." The court, in addressing prong two, however, identified that Policy 227 called for a strict protocol and the collection of samples by trained medical personnel in a discreet manner. Furthermore, the court cited the fact that a negative test resulted in no other penalty than suspension from the activity. It was also important for the court to point out that Policy 227 involved adequate notice on the possibility for drug testing.

The court took major issue with the third prong of the test—the nature and immediacy of the governmental concern and the

High school students attend an antidrug rally in Boston. Many students are in favor of random student drug testing.

efficacy of the means employed to address that concern. The majority found that the District's policy was based on the general deterrence of drug use and failed to establish the existence of a specific drug problem in the District or with the targeted group of students. Furthermore, the court found no evidence to suggest that the policy would address any drug problems the District may have. This included a lack of proof that the target group included drug users or "leaders in the drug culture," and seemed to actually ignore those students most likely to take part in drug use. Due to the lack of specific evidence presented by the District, the court held that Policy 227 did not meet the article I, section 8 requirements.

Don't Wait for a Tragedy

The Pennsylvania Supreme Court's decision in *Theodore* , although commendable in its attempt to preserve individual rights and foster the ideas of state sovereignty, is troubling in two distinct ways. First, the court has sent a message that preemptive problem solving is unavailable to school districts in their fight against teenage drug use. The United States Supreme Court in *Earls* stated that "the nationwide drug epidemic makes the war against drugs a pressing concern in every school." The Pennsylvania Supreme Court, itself, noted the importance of preemptive problem solving in *In re F.B.* when it stated that "[s]chools are simply 'not required to wait for a tragedy to occur within their walls to demonstrate that the need is immediate.'" In *Theodore*, the court attempted to distinguish the threat of weapons from that presented by drug use. The fact is, both guns and drugs are extremely dangerous and become increasingly more dangerous in the hands of teenagers. As the concurring opinion points out, the need for measures preventing drug use is as intrinsic in the importance of maintaining school safety and effectiveness as the need to avert weapons possession by students. The immediacy of the danger may weigh in favor of weapons, but in terms of overall and continued risk, drug use seems to be at least equivalent with the possession of weapons. . . .

Get the Community Involved

It is crucial that all members of the community and especially those affected by the policy (students and parents) have at least some form of notice and the opportunity to object to the policy. This opportunity could be as extensive as a parent "input night," or as basic as providing copies of the policy and its purposes to each student and his or her parents in order to inform them before they sign a contract indicating their acknowledgement and consent to testing. In providing such an opportunity, a lack of strong disapproval or refusal to consent would impliedly indicate that the community (parents) was concerned, as well, with the possible increasing problem (depending on the purposes for the program that are stated in the notice) presented by drugs or alcohol in the district's schools.

Uniformity Is Important

Secondly, without delving too far into the concepts of new federalism, it is important to note that the court's decision hinders any attempt at uniformity and clarity under the United States Constitution and also, in a narrower sense, under the state constitution. . . . In theory, new federalism is an exercise of state sovereignty, but in practicality, however, it has led to a "perplexing melange of disparate constitutional principles." In other words, there is a possibility for fifty different approaches to one issue, creating "an almost limitless number of variations and permutations." This presents a troubling scenario where citizens of the United States will be treated differently under the Constitution depending on their state of residence. . . .

The rule enunciated by the court that "a search policy will pass constitutional scrutiny only if the District makes some actual showing of the specific need for the policy and an explanation of its basis for believing that the policy would address that need," also creates an unintelligible threshold. . . . This . . . will not only cause the Pennsylvania common pleas courts to continually attempt to guess at the adequate level of evidence needed, but, more importantly, makes it nearly impossible for a school district to develop a policy that they could be relatively certain would not be invalidated. This will of course lead to increased litigation as the policies are challenged.

TEN

A Student Against Drug Testing

Amanda Gelender

Amanda Gelender is a student activist and one of ten high school seniors honored by the American Civil Liberties Union (ACLU) in 2005. Gelender organized a chapter of Students for Sensible Drug Policy at Castro Valley High School in California and wrote numerous articles on civil liberties in her school newspaper. She currently attends Stanford University. In the following article, she writes that drug testing is immoral, unconstitutional, and a waste of educational dollars.

The summer before my junior year at Castro Valley High School, I embarked on a journey that changed my life. It was a week-long student field-investigation (sponsored by the ACLU's Howard A. Friedman First Amendment Education Project) to study the "war on drugs." I went on the trip with little knowledge of drug policy and came out an educated activist for drug policy reform. When I returned to school in the fall, I started a chapter of Students for Sensible Drug Policy, despite extreme opposition. And when the Drug Policy Alliance contacted me to testify for SB 1386, which would ban random drug testing in California public high schools, I readily accepted. Testifying in Sacramento alongside the amazing Glenn Backes and Marsha Rosenbaum from the Alliance was one of the highlights of my young life.

Amanda Gelender, "Student Speaks Out on Drug Testing," www.drugpolicy.org, March 9, 2005. Reproduced by permission of the author.

Trust Is Compromised

I believe that random drug testing is immoral, unconstitutional, degrading, and inefficient. First and foremost, I am a student, not a criminal. I should not be treated as a suspect and policed by my educators. I have a lot of respect for my teachers, and I am confident that the trusting relationships I have developed with them would decay if they listened outside a bathroom stall while I peed into a cup. Students have the fourth amendment right to privacy, and random drug testing leads students to a warped understanding of the Bill of Rights, specifically freedom from unreasonable searches.

Tests Are Unreliable

Not only is drug testing a gross waste of precious education funds, but the tests are ineffective. Drug tests don't reveal whether a student smoked one joint a month ago or takes bong hits between

A police officer handles a drug-sniffing dog in a classroom. Some students believe such measures promote a negative school environment.

URINALYSIS

classes. They may not detect binge drinking, although alcohol is the most widely used drug among high school students. It's also ridiculously easy to outsmart the tests, especially with clean urine samples from peers or for purchase. Conversely, students can be victims of false positives as a result of ingesting a poppy seed muffin or a decongestant.

There Is a Better Way

If the ultimate goal is to steer students away from illicit drug use, then counseling programs, extra-curricular activities, supportive teachers, and involved parents are the solution. But when money for books goes toward drug tests, educators turn into police officers, and communication and honesty is substituted with urine samples, then something has gone terribly wrong with our education system.

ELEVEN

A Student for Drug Testing

Tamara Pollock

> Portage Area High School in Pennsylvania has four hundred students. Three hundred are voluntarily in a student drug testing program. Tamara Pollock actively advocates for voluntary drug testing at her high school. She holds several leadership positions, including captain of the varsity cheerleading squad, an officer of the band, a member of the track team, and an executive council member of Students Against Destructive Decisions (SADD).

Simply being a teen puts me under an enormous amount of pressure. The pressures to succeed, to do well, and to please others are just a few that I have had to deal with. I believe taking part in our drug screening gives me, along with other students, a reason to say no and a reason to stand up for what we believe, which is being drug and alcohol free! I am proud to belong to the program because it gives me a way to show that I am not embarrassed about my decisions.

Testing Is a Deterrent

At Portage High School, any student has the opportunity to be drug screened. I think that because we have this opportunity it helps keep students away from drugs and alcohol. Knowing that I can be tested at any time makes me scared to even try a little bit of something. I love cheering and I know that if I were ever to fail a random test, I would no longer be cheering. I know this policy makes others feel the same way.

Testing Identifies Who Needs Help

The main reason I agree with the random student drug screening is because I know some of my peers do use drugs and drink alcohol and they need help. People start using for many reasons you and I may not understand. I believe that in some sort of way these people are crying out for help. I do not blame their problems entirely on them. Peer pressure is hard to deal with and sometimes wrong choices are made. The ultimate thing with the random student drug screening is to discover the problem and help the person. Addiction is difficult to deal with and I know getting away from it is one of the hardest things a person can do in their lifetime.

Doug Marlette for *Newsday*. Reproduced by permission.

A teenage girl talks with a physician. Random drug testing can save lives and gives teens a way to stand up to peer pressure.

Testing Can Save Lives

I know that random drug screening can possibly save someone's life. I have a really close friend who has an addiction. At one point things were getting extremely bad but he got caught. He got help and I stuck beside him through it all. I want him to get better. He is now involved in the random drug screening, which helps and motivates him. People are there for him and are giving him more insight on the hazards. Although he is not completely clean, having people who are there for him helps a great deal. Random drug screening is one of the best things the school offers. I believe it can ultimately save a person's life.

TWELVE

Drug Tests Are Easily Outsmarted

Amitava Dasgupta

In the following testimony Amitava Dasgupta describes the challenge posed by efforts to cheat on drug tests. In 1988, just two years after federally mandated drug testing commenced, common household chemicals were used to "beat" the test. These half-dozen chemicals, when added to a positive urine specimen, were effective in producing a negative result. Products to beat the test are easy to obtain over the Internet, at retail stores, or via toll-free telephone numbers. Amitava Dasgupta is recognized as an expert in drug testing. Dasgupta is professor of pathology and laboratory medicine at the University of Texas Health Sciences Center at Houston and has written dozens of papers and contributed chapters to two books on the topic of substance abuse.

On September 15, 1986, President [Ronald] Reagan issued Executive Order No. 12564 directing federal agencies to achieve a drug free work environment. Then the Department of Health and Human Services developed guidelines for drugs of abuse testing. In the military where the urine collection process is supervised, chances of an adulterated specimen are remote but in pre-employment testing where direct supervision of specimen collection is not practiced, a person may attempt to beat a drug

Amitava Dasgupta, "Kits to Circumvent Drug Tests," testimony to U.S. Committee on House Energy and Commerce, Subcommittee on Oversight and Investigations, Washington, D.C., May 17, 2005.

test by adulterating the specimen. Reports of usage of household chemicals such as bleach, table salt, laundry detergent, toilet bowl cleaner, vinegar, lemon juice and Visine eye drops for adulterating urine specimens were published in medical literature as early as 1988. Most of these adulterants except Visine eye drops can be detected by routine specimen integrity tests.

More recently a variety of products are commercially available which can be ordered either through the Internet sites or toll free numbers. Synthetic urine is premixed urine with all the characteristic of natural urine. The product can be heated in a microwave oven for up to 10 seconds in order to achieve a temperature between 90 to 100F [degrees].

Urine is tested for the presence of illegal drugs. Many people cheat on drug tests to avoid a positive result.

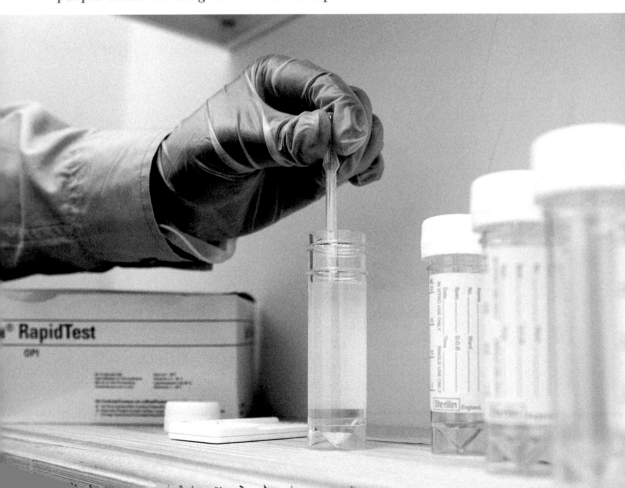

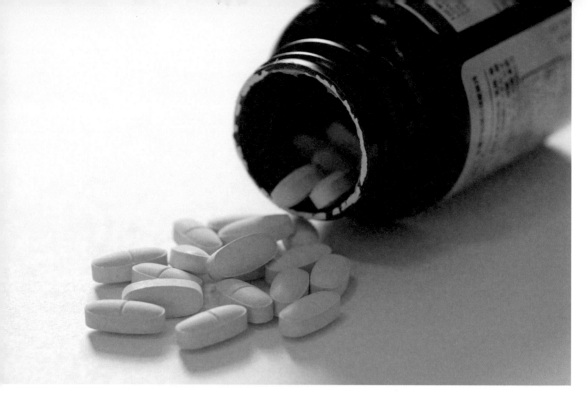

Commercial products such as these herbal pills can create a false negative on a drug test by removing traces of drugs from urine.

Commercially available products to beat drug tests can be classified under two broad categories. The first category is taking specific fluids or tablets along with plenty of water to flush out drugs and metabolites. Many of these products can produce dilute urine and the concentrations of drugs or metabolites can be significantly reduced. The second category of products available is in vitro urinary adulterants, which should be added to urine after collection in order to pass a drug test. Urinary adulterants [are] available through the Internet.

Negative Results Don't Mean "Drug-free"

A negative result for the presence of abused drugs in a urine specimen does not mean that no drug was present. It is also possible that the amount of drug was below the cut-off values used in the drug testing protocol. Diluting urine is a simple way to beat otherwise positive drug tests if the original concentrations of drugs in the urine are moderate. Use of flushing and detoxification is frequently advertised as an effective means to pass drug tests. Published reports indicate that diuretic[s] can cause false negative results due to diluted urine.

Laboratories routinely check pH, temperature, specific gravity and creatinine of urine to detect validity of specimens. Although adulteration with common household compounds can be detected by this mechanism, the presence of newer urine adulterants cannot be detected by urine specimen integrity tests.

Masking Agents Are Effective

Wu et al. reported that the active ingredient of [one product] is 200 mmol/L of pyridinium chlorochromate (PCC). This product may help beat drug tests for marijuana and opiates. Other products contain potassium nitite and are effective in masking moderate concentrations of marijuana metabolites from detection by immunoassays or gas chromatography/mass spectrometry. [Another product] consists of two vials, one containing a powder (peroxidase) and another vial containing a liquid (hydrogen peroxide). Both products should be added to the urine specimen. [This] is capable of producing false negative results using immunoassay methods when marijuana metabolites, LSD and opiates (morphine) were present in the urine at 125–150% of cutoff values. Glutaraldehyde has also been used as an adulterant to mask urine drug tests. . . . Glutaraldehyde at a concentration of 0.75% volume can lead to false negative screening results for marijuana tests using immunoassays. At higher concentrations (1–2%) amphetamine, methadone, benzodiazepine, opiate and cocaine metabolite tests are also affected. The presence of [newer urine adulterants] can be detected in adulterated urine specimens by various spot tests. Recently, on-site adulterant detection devices are commercially available.

Hair and saliva specimens are alternatives to urine specimens for drug testing. Several products are available for sale through the Internet that claim washing hair with these shampoos can aid a person to pass a drug test. Saliva samples are also used for drug testing. A mouthwash is available commercially claiming that rinsing the mouth twice with this product can help a person to beat saliva based drug testing which is often a popular method of testing by insurance companies. However, effectiveness of such products in beating drug tests has not been clearly established by scientific research.

New Adulterants Require New Tests

In conclusion, adulterants impose a new challenge in the testing for abused drugs. Routine specimen integrity testing is not adequate to detect the presence of more recently introduced adulterants which may effectively mask modest amounts of abused drugs from detection. Intake of herbal cleansing agents and diuretics may also aid a person to beat drug tests by producing diluted urine with reduced concentrations of drugs.

THIRTEEN

A Sense of Belonging Reduces Student Drug Use

Robert Blum

In the following selection Robert Blum argues that school connectedness—a sense of bonding, attachment, owner-ship, participation, and belonging—lowers the risk of ille-gal drug use. While school connectedness includes peer rela-tionships, research indicates that relationships between students and adults at school may be even more significant. Students are best protected against risky behavior when they feel that the adults in the school care about them per-sonally. High school is particularly crucial: By the time stu-dents reach this level, 40 to 60 percent have emotionally disconnected from school. That figure does not include those who have permanently disconnected by dropping out of school. School connectedness can be dramatically improved when students, parents, teachers, and staff make a conscious and collective decision to make a change. The more positive and caring relationships students have at school, the lower their risk for illegal drug use. Robert Blum is the William H. Gates Sr. Professor and Chair, Department of Population and Family Health Sciences, Johns Hopkins Bloomberg School of Public Health, and is nationally rec-ognized as an expert on school connectedness.

Research has shown that students who feel connected to school do better academically and also are less likely to be involved in risky health behaviors: drug use, cigarette smoking, early sex, violence and suicidal thoughts and attempts. This report summarizes what is known about school connectedness. School connection is the belief by students that adults in the school care about their learning and about them as individuals. Students are more likely to succeed when they feel connected to school. Critical requirements for feeling connected include high academic rigor and expectations coupled with support for learning, positive adult-student relationships, and physical and emotional safety.

Young people who feel a sense of belonging and connectedness at school are less likely to become involved with drugs and alcohol.

Increasing the number of students connected to school is likely to improve critical accountability measures. Strong scientific evidence demonstrates that increased student connection to school decreases absenteeism, fighting, bullying and vandalism while promoting educational motivation, classroom engagement, academic performance, school attendance and completion rates.

Connectedness Equals Success

In order to succeed, students need to feel they "belong" in their school. People call that sense of belonging many things. Some researchers study "school engagement" while others study "school attachment," and still others analyze "school bonding." To complicate matters even more, research on students' attachment to the schools they attend is conducted in a variety of disciplines: education, health, psychology and sociology. Are all these people talking about the same thing?

By and large, the answer is yes. While each discipline may organize data and terms differently, conduct analyses in different ways, and even use different descriptive words, consistent themes emerge. These seven qualities seem to influence students' positive attachment to school:

- Having a sense of belonging and being part of a school
- Liking school
- Perceiving that teachers are supportive and caring
- Having good friends within school
- Being engaged in their own current and future academic progress
- Believing that discipline is fair and effective
- Participating in extracurricular activities

These factors, measured in different ways, are highly predictive of success in school. Because each of these seven factors brings with it a sense of connection—to oneself, one's community or one's friends—it is clear that school connectedness makes a difference in the lives of American youth.

In the healthy development of children and youth, grades, participation, a sense of belonging, and relationships with students

Many teenagers feel disengaged from high school, which can produce feelings of loneliness and depression.

and teachers are important in feeling connected to school—and connected students do better. There are those who believe that schools should focus only on the acquisition of knowledge or that we expect too much from schools. However, current research across disciplines shows that non-academic aspects of school are also significant contributors to both school and student success. . . .

Relationships Are the Key

Individuals create school connectedness. By the time they are in high school, as many as 40 to 60 percent of all students—urban, suburban and rural—are chronically disengaged from school. That disturbing number does not include the young people who have already dropped out. What is behind this serious disengagement, and what can be done about it?

First, we must recognize that *people connect with people* before they connect with institutions. The relationships formed between students and school staff members are at the heart of school connectedness. Students who perceive their teachers and school administrators as creating a caring, well-structured learning environment in which expectations are high, clear and fair are more likely to be connected to school.

But it is not just teachers and administrators who create these important connections. Janitors, coaches, lunchroom servers, office assistants, counselors, parents and school volunteers—in short, all adults—are critically important in this dynamic.

Simply put, when we create more personalized educational environments, students respond and do better. Teachers report and research confirms that connected students pay better attention, stay focused, are motivated to do more than required, and tend to have higher grades and test scores.

Promoting Positive Outcomes

As any 21st century teacher will attest, schools can be either a positive or negative force in a student's life. Sometimes, it's a matter of young people connecting to less-than-desirable models. Parents have believed for decades that young people who build strong social connections to individuals who engage in risky behaviors are more likely to take the same risks. These parents are appropriately concerned—and they are right.

School connectedness, however, has been shown to protect youth from engaging in risky behaviors. The health benefits of positive versus negative behaviors are obvious. Across all racial, ethnic and income groups, evidence is mounting that students who feel more connected to school are less likely to:

• Exhibit disruptive and violent behavior
• Carry or use a weapon

- Experiment with illegal substances
- Smoke cigarettes
- Drink to the point of getting drunk
- Appear emotionally distressed
- Consider or attempt suicide
- Engage in early-age sexual intercourse

Teachers Are Paramount

Peer social acceptance alone does not protect students from risk. Children must be taught in ways that motivate, engage and involve them in learning. Critical to that is the relationship between the teacher and the student. Indeed, teacher support is essential in guiding students toward positive, productive behaviors. This relationship allows students to develop a stake in their own achievement.

Effective teachers use proactive management strategies. They establish consistent classroom expectations and routines, and they recognize and reward desirable student behavior. They help students set both academic and behavioral goals, share the goals with parents, and review them periodically.

Effective teachers use interactive and experiential teaching methods that are oriented to explicit learning objectives. They develop assignments in which students investigate issues, interview people, visit sites and report back to the teacher. They involve small teams of students of different ability levels and recognize the academic improvement of individual team members.

These teachers become a creative, energizing force in the learning process, and their importance cannot be overestimated. Many individuals credit their adult success to one caring, inspiring teacher they had as a youth. . . .

Participation Is Essential

School is the business of youth, and administrators and teachers can do much to improve students' sense of connectedness.

Students must also actively participate in their own education. They need opportunities to become involved in cross-age and

A teacher who maintains a positive relationship with students is crucial to providing young people with a sense of belonging at school.

peer-led tutoring activities, serve as peer counselors, experience collaborative learning that pairs stronger and weaker students, and participate in new-student orientation programs, buddy programs and welcome programs.

Likewise, parents and community members can contribute to the success of the school. They can serve as mentors, participate in or provide opportunities for community service, take advantage of parent training opportunities, develop ongoing relationships between the school and corporations or universities, and provide opportunities for and participate in service learning.

Students Should Feel Safe

Schools are responsible for providing students with a safe environment in which to develop academically, emotionally and behaviorally. One element of the school environment is the school "climate," which, at its most positive, includes a strong emphasis on academic achievement, positive relationships among students and teachers, respect for all members of the school community, fair and consistent discipline policies, attention to safety issues, and family and community involvement.

At a youth workshop, teens learn the importance of building self-confidence and leadership skills as a way of avoiding negative peer pressure.

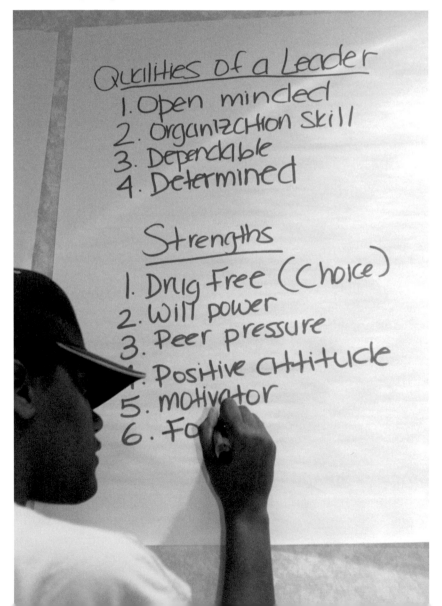

School climate and connectedness are interrelated. School climate, positive or negative, affects students' sense of safety and their risk for delinquency. Students will actively avoid schools that have an unpleasant climate or schools where they feel out of place. A negative school climate also increases risks for serious violent behavior.

Researchers, however, point to some good news. When students, teachers, staff and parents collectively and consciously decide to improve a school environment, successful climate change is possible.

The greater the sense of school connectedness among students, the more positive is the school climate. School connectedness is akin to social bonding. When students feel connected to school, they are able to develop positive relationships with adults, increase involvement in positive behaviors, avoid behaviors that harm their health, and buffer the effects of risky environments such as violence or drug use at home. . . .

In any organization, there is no substitute for capable, motivational leadership. Schools are no exception. School administrators and teachers set the tone, provide behavioral examples and establish a climate of trust or mistrust. . . .

Learn to Manage Emotions

Social and emotional learning (SEL) is the name given to programs with the common goal of teaching students how to manage emotions, develop caring and concern for others, make responsible decisions, establish positive relationships and effectively handle challenging situations. Effective programs must teach students the five essential social and emotional learning skill areas: self-awareness, social awareness, self-management, relationship skills and responsible decision-making. They focus on the themes of self-discipline, respect, and responsibility to self and others. Programs include professional development, which extends beyond an initial workshop to include on-site observation and coaching. The Chicago School District has recently included SEL goals as part of its school report card measures.

Learn Social Skills

Project Northland, a three-year program starting in the sixth grade, is designed to prevent alcohol and cigarette use. Student skills-training includes enhancing competence in relating to parents, handling peers/peer pressure, and creating normal expectations about alcohol. Schools use a social behavioral curriculum, homework, peer leadership training and media, and they involve parents in the education. Community-wide task forces in 20 school districts in Minnesota have used this curriculum. By the end of eighth grade, intervention district schools had lower alcohol, marijuana and cigarette use.

Student Cliques Are Powerful

An individual school's culture represents a balance of priorities between social needs and learning. While learning might be the priority of teachers, students have many other reasons to come to school. For some, socializing, sports and extracurricular activities are at least as important as learning. Likewise, being athletic, funny, friendly, outgoing, attractive and popular are more important achievements for some students than being "smart" or getting good grades.

The social needs of students are often dictated and met by the cliques with whom they associate. In most schools, cliques represent stereotypes, and status is measured by a "cool factor." Identities as jocks, preppies and populars may carry prestige and bring power. Freaks, goths, losers, druggies and nerds may be at the bottom of the status hierarchy. Most students actually fall between these extremes, and if a school has several leading cliques, a single group is less able to impose their norms on everybody else.

The views, values and actions of the popular clique and its leadership, however, are particularly powerful in defining the culture of a school. If these values embrace fun over future, sports over studies or popularity over productivity, they will undermine a pro-learning environment. An anti-learning culture is also likely to develop if students believe that teachers and the classroom are a

By promoting a sense of connectedness and unity, extracurricular activities and interests offer a positive way for students to socialize.

"game" in which teachers pick winners and losers but do not provide something for everyone. . . .

Health Education Helps

Because of the strong link between school connectedness and reductions in health risk behaviors, many health promotion programs aim to increase school connectedness. Although few such health programs have been rigorously evaluated, available evidence points to common elements of effective programs. What is clear is that effective health promotion programs go beyond the specific messages they teach to help young people to view themselves, their bodies and the people with whom they relate in a different and more positive manner. . . .

Effective school-based health promotion programs also share the following characteristics. They:

- Ensure consistency and clarity in policies and messages
- Involve students as leaders and reward positive student behavior
- Provide positive adult role models and opportunities for family connections
- Ensure school commitment and support at all levels
- Use interactive programs that enhance development of interpersonal skills
- Conduct life skills training, including refusal and resistance skills, decision making, goal setting, assertiveness, bullying prevention, coping and communication
- Increase awareness about media and advertising influences, particularly regarding substance use and abuse
- Avoid short-term interventions but employ multi-setting interventions, including school, family, media and community

Parents Learn with Youth

Project STAR/Midwestern Prevention Project reduces drug use by working with students over a five-year period. The school component involves 20 hours of direct contact with students and parents in years one and two, focusing on resisting and countering drug use. A mass media campaign is also included. Fifty middle/junior high schools in 15 communities were evaluated, although not all sites received all the components of the program. Six years after intervention, drug use among students who participated in the program was lower than drug use in those who did not participate.

Current research shows great promise for policies and programs that will further enhance the concept of school connectedness.

FOURTEEN

Drug Tests Can Promote a Sense of Belonging

Ashley Coffman

> In 1998 the 110th-largest school district in the United States, the Winston-Salem Forsyth County Schools in North Carolina, began drug testing its students after surveys of seventeen hundred high school students in Kernersville found that 92 percent of the respondents believed that "in my school most students use drugs." Students who enroll in the drug testing program are given prizes, incentives, parties, and newspaper recognition. The Forsyth County sheriff's office paid for the drug testing. In the following excerpt Ashley Coffman argues that the program has caused a positive shift in peer pressure. At school, the drug-free majority teamed up and started promoting its viewpoints. The result is that about 75 percent of middle and high school students in Kernersville are in the testing program each year. Drug testing and incentives have been a catalyst for increased connectedness among students, parents, teachers, businesses, police, and town officials. Ashley Coffman is a recent graduate of North Carolina State University and a staff reporter for the *Kernersville News*.

"I don't have a problem letting people know I don't do drugs," said Matt Baker, an eleventh grade athlete at East Forsyth High School (EFHS).

Elementary school students participate in an antidrug rally.

According to Roman Nelson, an EFHS tenth grader, signing the pledge to be drug-free and agreeing to random drug-testing "is a good way to publicize that you are against drugs."

Testing Is Promoted by Students

At EFHS, the program is student led and 68 percent of the student body is signed up. Sarah Edwards, a senior at EFHS and the KCK (Kernersville Cares for Kids)/Students Against Violence Everywhere president, said, "Teachers don't pressure you. It's the student's decision."

According to a group of six individuals interviewed at EFHS, it is not a big deal to be drug tested. Michael Coleman, EFHS senior class president, said he had been drug tested and there was total privacy on his end. Coleman said he was not nervous about being drug tested because he knew he was drug free. "The lady was very nice," he said. Coleman further explained that his experience during drug testing seemed normal and "they don't try to make you feel bad."

Testing Promotes Unity

The conclusion one might draw from talking with EFHS [students] involved in KCK is that joining the club and agreeing to random student drug testing appears to be a catalyst for bringing them, the community, along with parents and teachers, together.

"It's the first step," said Kernersville Police (KPD) Chief Neal Stockton. "Students make a statement to be drug free, keep their life clean, and not be subject to abusing drugs."

"I think the pledge itself shows that they are a majority, not a minority," said Stockton. "It's like peer pressure in reverse. It's

Drug-Free Pledge

I pledge allegiance to myself and who I want to be,
'Cause I can make my dreams come true if I believe in me.
I pledge to stay in school and learn the things I need to know,
To make the world a better place for kids like me to grow.
I pledge to keep my dreams alive and be all I can be
I know I can, and that's because I pledge to stay Drug-Free!

Source: Partnership for a Drug-Free America, www.drugfree.org.

where you have people with a positive forecast on life coming to the forefront, saying I am going to be drug free."

According to Stockton, those students who pledge to be drug-free empower people who may be hesitant about making a statement about being drug-free. Saying "No" is the hardest thing for a young person to do, according to Stockton. "Saying no now is fashionable in the fact that they can stand for a stronger voice."

That stronger voice, according to Stockton, is the silent majority which has come forward to sign the pledge to say no. Stockton further explained that during high school students start to "look at things with a different eye."

Testing Prepares Students for Jobs

Students realize that no one wants to hire someone with a drug dependency. "Joining this program and signing the pledge is a character building opportunity," said Stockton.

"In a lot of jobs you have to get drug tested," said Coleman, who further explained that starting a program like this now prepares them for the future.

KCK Rewards Students

Not only do the students rally behind one another's decisions, they provide incentives to reward those students who commit to be drug-free. For example, at EFHS classes with 100 percent participation in the "It's My Call" [and "It's Our Call" drug testing] program will be able to participate in a biscuit breakfast. ["It's My Call" is voluntary, but all students involved in extracurricular activities must enroll in "It's Our Call."]

The community and KCK often provide incentives for the students. The KPD raises funds to purchase incentives and local restaurants donate or reduce the cost of food for this cause.

"It takes a community to raise a child," said Helen Prince, EFHS teacher and coordinator for "It's My Call" at EFHS. "It takes everyone working together. Being drug-free creates a safe environment."

According to Prince, the community has given incentives as a means of recognizing students who have taken a stand to be drug-free. As a teacher, Prince said, "Anything we can do is beneficial. If we can save one child then it's been worth the program."

Police Bond with Students

Threatening adolescents with police officers is an issue of the past, according to Stockton. He continued by saying there is now a pro-police attitude in middle schools. [Each middle school and each

These students have a positive relationship with law enforcement officers. Such a bond is an important weapon against teen drug use.

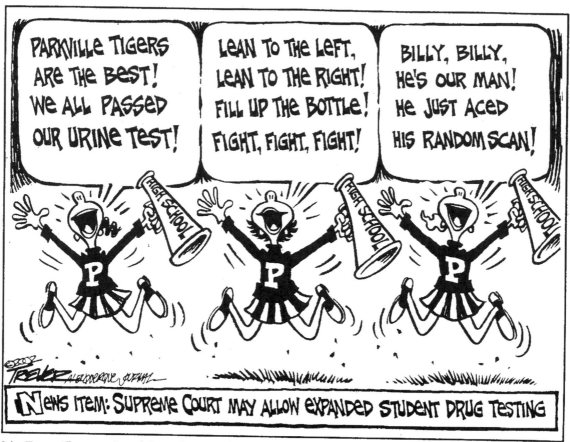

John Trever, *Albuquerque Journal*. Copyright © 2002 by Trever. Reproduced by permission.

high school employs a full-time school resource officer.] "Kids walk by with a thumbs up; that signifies they are cool with police officers," he said. "Police are there to do more than just put handcuffs on someone."

In this case, the KPD has been very involved with the KCK program. The department's involvement gives students an opportunity to talk openly about drug addiction and drug abuse.

Testing Is Voluntary at Middle School

In middle schools, signing the pledge is strictly voluntary. It is not required for students involved in sports nor is it required of those in extracurricular activities, according to Southeast Middle School (SEMS) Principal Debbie Blanton-Warren.

In the "It's My Call" program at SEMS, 87 percent of the students are signed up. "We are a lot like a big family here," said Annie Orchard, KCK president at SEMS. "We are like brothers and sisters so we encourage each other to be drug-free just like brothers and sisters do." The students at SEMS have united together in this program and seem very close to the students involved in the program.

Peer Pressure Is Positive

"This makes us feel like a team," said Jordyn Reisenaver, an eighth grader at Southeast Middle School. "Like we are fighting drugs together."

At a young age, when peer pressure is a big part of life, this program allows students involved to share a common ground to promote positive peer pressure. "People will sign up if a lot of the students sign up," said Reisenaver. "We say that we are signed up, then they are not afraid to sign up."

The students at SEMS said it is also fun to promote being drug-free at their school. "We made it part of School Spirit Week," said Warren. "We had a day where we wore our T-shirts and bracelets and about 70 percent of the kids participated."

Government Supports Local Program

A drug testing grant worth nearly $800,000 was presented to the Winston-Salem/Forsyth County School System by the nation's Drug Czar John Walters, who was accompanied by the Deputy Secretary of the US Department of Education, Ray Simon, at the national press conference for the Office of National Drug [Control] Policy held at Carver High School in Winston-Salem on Wednesday, October 19 [2005].

According to Kathy Jordan, program specialist for Safe and Drug-Free Schools in the Winston-Salem/Forsyth County School System, "Drug testing is a means of achieving a broader goal."

Testing Connects Choices with Consequences

The program "gives you that ripple effect," according to Stockton. "Take care of one problem, then it will take care of several other problems."

According to Stockton, student drug testing is a stepping stone. "It leads to a better citizenship and shows accountability and responsibility at a young age to be learning that you've put your name on something that carries some weight. I like that," he said.

"It is just one piece of the pie and an important piece in terms of accountability, but the larger goal is to create the opportunity for a student to identify with the process of being drug-free, not just to catch kids with positive test results," said Jordan.

"With every choice you take there are consequences and this is an opportunity for them to make a positive choice with positive consequences," said Stockton.

What You Should Know About Student Drug Testing

Facts About Standard Student Drug Testing

- In 2002 the United States Supreme Court ruled that suspicion-less drug testing for students involved in extracurricular activities is constitutional.
- One in five schools uses some form of drug testing.

The Office of National Drug Control Policy Has Established the Following Guidelines for Schools Considering Starting an SDT Program:

- The school must have a written student drug-testing (SDT) policy that
  1. establishes the need for an SDT program;
  2. states the school's position on substance abuse, student health and safety, confidentiality, and how this relates to the SDT program;
  3. outlines the program, such as what groups of students will be tested, how they will be selected, what drugs will be tested for, how test specimens will be collected, how parental and student consent will be obtained, how confidentiality will be protected, and the consequences for a positive (failed) test or refusal to take the test;
  4. clearly states students' rights and the school's responsibilities.

- Students and parents must sign a consent form stating that they have received a copy of the school's written drug policy, understand it, and are willing to take part in the drug-testing program.
- A positive (failed) suspicionless drug test will not affect a student's grades or academic standing.
- A positive suspicionless drug test will not be a part of a student's permanent record, as all drug-testing data and test results are destroyed upon graduation or departure from the school district. Results are confidential and will not affect a student's chances of going to college.
- Law enforcement will not be notified of the results of a suspicionless drug test.
- The consequence of a positive test result for illicit drugs is directly related to the extracurricular activities in which the student engages. Some schools may limit or prohibit participation, while other schools allow students to continue to participate as long as they attend and complete counseling/treatment. Each school designs its own written policy.
- A positive test result will be confirmed at a state-licensed or federally certified lab using spectrometry.
- A certified medical review officer (MRO) will review the confirmed-positive test to determine if there exists a legitimate reason for the positive result, such as a drug prescribed to the student. If the positive is due to a legitimate reason, it will be reported as a negative and the school is not informed of the prescription drug use.
- Confidentiality is an integral part of any SDT program. The MRO will notify the student, parents/legal guardians, and the principal. In most cases only the principal and the superintendent have access to the test results at school.
- A school must have a clear protocol for working with students who test positive for illicit drugs. It is common for schools to have a Student Assistance Program (SAP) which connects students with appropriate local agencies to help them resolve underlying problems such as family conflicts, depression, learning disabilities, illness, isolation, or substance abuse.

- A student is never forced to take a suspicionless drug test. However, if a student declines the test, the student is ineligible for extracurricular activities until he/she complies with the drug-testing policy. Each school designs its own written policy.
- A school must use a reliable lab and a reliable test. The school is responsible for knowing the accuracy of the lab and tests.
- The number of drugs and the type of drugs tested for will affect the cost of the test. The standard five-panel screen tests for marijuana, cocaine, opiates, PCP, and amphetamines. Schools can design a test panel specific to the drugs most commonly abused in their community, including alcohol, steroids, and club drugs.
- In a random testing program, the testing must be random. Students may not be singled out; instead, names must be pooled and randomly drawn.
- Parents are notified each time a student is tested, and the results are shared with them.
- Student drug-testing programs are funded by grants through the Department of Education's Office of Safe and Drug-Free Schools, asset-forfeiture funds from drug raids, nonprofit organizations, local businesses, activity fees charged to parents or subsidized by the athletic booster club, or by other means.
- If a school decides to test all of its students or students other than those permitted by the Court, then the school must be prepared to go to court to prove that the testing is constitutional.
- While the purpose of student drug testing is to deter drug use and help students who use drugs, *possession* of drugs often results in punishment. Possession of drugs on school property makes any student subject to the school's written drug policy, which may include being expelled and reported to law enforcement. These outcomes could affect the student's college prospects.

General Facts About Teenage Drug Use
- According to the 2005 *Monitoring the Future Survey*, by eighth grade 21 percent of students have used illicit drugs. By twelfth grade 50 percent of students have used illicit drugs.

- Marijuana is the illicit drug most used by teens.
- OxyContin and Vicodin, prescription painkillers, are the fastest-growing drugs of abuse among high school students.
- The average age for first experimentation with marijuana is thirteen years, and about 75 percent of students who have *ever* used marijuana are still using it in twelfth grade.
- According to the National Center on Addiction and Substance Abuse at Columbia University, the earlier a student uses drugs, the greater the likelihood of dependence on those substances and of academic failure.
- According to the 2005 *Monitoring the Future Survey*, 2.6 percent of seniors, 2 percent of tenth graders, and 1.7 percent of eighth graders have tried steroids.

General Facts About Student Risk for Drug Use

- Teens who attend schools where drugs are used, kept, or sold are three times likelier to have tried marijuana than teens who attend drug-free schools.
- From 2004 to 2005 the number of teens who knew a friend or classmate that abused prescription drugs increased 86 percent.
- Teens who believe that it is "not morally wrong" for someone their age to use marijuana are nineteen times more likely to use marijuana than teens who believe it is "seriously morally wrong."
- Twenty-one percent of twelve- to seventeen-year-olds say they can buy marijuana in one hour or less, while 42 percent say they can buy marijuana within a day.
- Students' risk for using illicit drugs increases sharply if they are highly stressed, often bored, and have twenty-five dollars or more weekly spending money or if they have been physically or sexually abused, have a learning disability or eating disorder, or suffer from serious depression
- The most common reason that students give for not using drugs is that they do not want to lose the respect of their parents.

What You Should Do About Student Drug Testing

Before you do anything about student drug testing, do your homework. Find out what you believe and why you believe it. Then, you will be able to take your stand—for or against student drug testing— with conviction. Only then will your stand be powerful enough to make a difference in your life and in the lives of others.

Get to the Bottom of the Issue

Before you form an opinion about student drug testing, do some research into the underlying issue of illicit drug use. Drugs such as amphetamines, cocaine, ecstasy, heroin, marijuana, methamphetamines, OxyContin, and PCP have been around for over eighty years. Why are they now illegal or legal only with a prescription? What changed in science or government? Using books such as *Drugs and Controlled Substances: Information for Students*, you can quickly research the history of hundreds of drugs in about fifty different categories.

Some drugs such as aspirin and cough syrup are legal and can be bought without a prescription. Other drugs such as painkillers are legal when they are prescribed by a licensed physician. However, it is illegal to take a prescription drug not prescribed to you or to take it in a manner other than prescribed. Sometimes legality depends not on the drug, but on the person's age. For instance, nicotine is legal for people eighteen years or older and alcohol is legal for people at least twenty-one years old. Finally, some drugs such as cocaine, marijuana, and methamphetamines are always illegal to use, possess, or sell.

Consequences of breaking the drug laws can vary considerably. For instance, a first-time offender convicted of possessing five grams of crack cocaine—which will fit into a teaspoon—will receive a mandatory minimum sentence of five years without parole. In contrast, first-time offenders convicted of possessing up to twenty-eight grams of marijuana may be fined or sentenced to treatment or community service, depending on which state they are convicted in.

In any case, being convicted of a drug offense can affect your ability to pay for or to be admitted to college. Under the U.S. Higher Education Act of 1998, anyone convicted of a drug offense is ineligible for federal student loans for a minimum of a year and sometimes indefinitely. It is important to note that the consequences are different for failing a drug test as part of the routine student drug-testing program (which grants the student immunity from law enforcement) and failing a drug test when a student is suspected of being under the influence or in possession of drugs.

Understand Both Sides of the Issue

Often, students who choose to stay drug-free will enroll in student drug testing at school. However, some students who do not use drugs nevertheless opt out of the student drug-testing program. Other students who use illicit drugs consent to drug testing. Why? Student drug testing is a complex issue. It involves more than just drugs and the law. It involves rights, privacy, intention, intervention, consequences, and public opinion.

The arguments for and against student drug testing are well defined. Learn as much as you can about both sides of the issue before drawing your own conclusion. Start with resources supplied in this book. Read the article excerpts, then explore other avenues of research, such as the books and magazine articles listed in the For Further Research section. In addition, contact the organizations or Web sites found in the list of Organizations to Contact and review the facts listed in the What You Should Know About Student Drug Testing appendix. In addition to the resources in this book, you can also conduct research at your school or local library or on the Internet.

While reviewing pro and con arguments side-by-side, ask yourself key questions that—when answered—will reveal your position on student drug testing. For instance, what is more important, an individual's rights to privacy or the rights of a school to protect its students? Is student drug abuse primarily a health issue, a legal issue, or a safety issue? Does student drug testing enhance or inhibit the perception of trust and safety at school? Is student drug testing an effective way to identify students who need help, or is it a waste of educational dollars?

Reaching Out

Your voice as a student is very powerful. Your peers, your school, and your community want to know what students believe about student drug testing. Because you have invested the time to understand both sides of this issue you are in the best position to voice your opinion.

You can begin by talking to the people you see every day—parents, friends, teachers, neighbors, and others in your community. As you begin to attract like-minded individuals, you might help organize a task force comprising of students, parents, businesspeople, school officials, and others.

In some schools the students—either for or against student drug testing—have signed petitions or held respectful demonstrations. These efforts have attracted the attention of the news media and brought the issue of student drug testing to the forefront of their community. Other students have taken the initiative to write a letter to the editor of their local newspaper expressing their concerns. Still other students have contacted their local school board—as ultimately the decision whether or not to implement a student drug-testing program rests with them.

Changing Drug Policy

Drug policy can vary considerably from school to school. Read the written drug policy for your school, which is found in the student handbook. In your opinion, is the policy fair, effective, and appropriate? If not, can the policy be improved? If so, why not write a letter to the school board or form a task force to improve the policy?

Is your school considering a student drug-testing program or does it already have one? Ask to join the task force and personally review the proposed or current policy. Do you agree with the testing procedures and the consequences for a failed drug test? If you feel that they are unfair or inappropriate, offer an alternative.

In some schools student drug testing is punitive. Students may feel that it is designed to catch "bad" kids or to punish students who break the law. In these programs students who test positive for illegal drugs are prohibited from participation in extracurricular activities for a specified period of time until certain conditions are met. Other schools have student drug-testing policies that are nonpunitive and often viewed by students as helpful. In these schools, as long as the student accepts counseling or intervention, the student can continue to participate in sports and clubs. These schools often have a Student Assistance Program (SAP) to determine if students have learning disabilities, depression, or serious family problems that may be contributing to a substance abuse problem. If so, the students are given help to address these issues. SAP programs can even be put in place for schools without student drug-testing programs.

Which type of program does your school have, if any? Which type do you think is best? Do you see a need for change in drug policy at your school? Many students across the country have accepted personal responsibility for changing their school's drug policy. They have joined with like-minded individuals, designed a plan of action, and accomplished their goals. Like them, you can make a difference in your life and your school by taking personal action.

After Graduation

You may feel that after graduation the issue of student drug testing will no longer be relevant. But this is not the case. The odds are that when you go to work, you will be drug tested, as about 80 percent of corporations use some form of drug testing. Later, if you are like the majority of your peers, you will marry and have children. As a parent, you will most likely be faced with the issue of student drug testing again. Now is the time to consider this issue that concerns you.

American Civil Liberties Union (ACLU)
125 Broad St., 18th Fl., New York, NY 10004-2400
(212) 549-2500
e-mail: aclu@aclu.org
Web site: www.aclu.org

The ACLU is a national organization that works to defend Americans' civil rights guaranteed by the U.S. Constitution. It provides legal defense, research, and education. The ACLU opposes student drug testing on the grounds that it violates students' constitutional rights to be presumed innocent and to be free from unreasonable searches and seizures. Its publications include *Making Sense of Student Drug Testing: Why Educators Are Saying No*.

American Council for Drug Education (ACDE)
164 W. Seventy-fourth St., New York, NY 10023
(800) 488-DRUG (3784) • fax: (212) 595-2553
Web site: www.acde.org

The American Council for Drug Education informs the public about the harmful effects of abusing drugs and alcohol. It gives the public access to scientifically based, compelling prevention programs and materials. ACDE offers resources for parents, youth, educators, prevention professionals, employers, health care professionals, and other concerned community members who are working to help America's youth avoid the dangers of drug and alcohol abuse.

Canadian Centre on Substance Abuse (CCSA)
75 Albert St., Suite 300, Ottawa ON K1P 5E7 Canada
(613) 235-4048 • fax: (613) 235-8101
e-mail: admin@ccsa.ca
Web site: www.ccsa.ca

Established in 1988 by an act of parliament, CCSA works to minimize the harm associated with the use of alcohol, tobacco, and other drugs. It disseminates information on the nature, extent, and consequences of substance abuse; sponsors public debates on the topic; and supports organizations involved in substance abuse treatment, prevention, and educational programming. The centre publishes the newsletter *Action News* six times a year.

Cato Institute
1000 Massachusetts Ave. NW, Washington, DC 20001-5403
(202) 842-0200
e-mail: cato@cato.org
Web site: www.cato.org

The institute is a public policy research foundation dedicated to limiting the control of government and to protecting individual liberty. Cato strongly favors drug legalization and opposes student drug testing. It publishes the *Cato Journal* three times a year, the *Cato Policy Report* bimonthly, and various reports, policy briefings, and articles.

Dads and Mad Moms Against Drug Dealers (DAMMADD)
PO Box 95, Tioga Center, New York, NY 13845
(866) 326-6233 (DAMMADD)
e-mail: stevensteiner@dammadd.org
Web site: www.dammadd.org

DAMMADD is a grassroots antidrug organization founded to help fight against drugs in schools, businesses, and the community. It raises public awareness of the drug problem through personal testimonies, presentations, and news stories. It also pays rewards for tips that lead to the arrest and conviction of drug dealers. A library at its sister site contains antidrug and pro-student drug-testing videos and stories for instant viewing at www.americansfor drugfreeyouth.org.

Drug Enforcement Administration (DEA)
2401 Jefferson Davis Hwy., Alexandria, VA 22301
(202) 307-1000
Web site: www.usdoj.gov/dea

The DEA is the federal agency charged with enforcing the nation's drug laws. The agency concentrates on stopping the smuggling and distribution of narcotics in the United States and abroad. It publishes the *Drug Enforcement Magazine* three times a year. It also publishes the e-brochure *Student Drug Testing: What You Should Know*.

Drug Policy Foundation
4455 Connecticut Ave. NW, Suite B-500
Washington, DC 20008-2328
(202) 537-5005 • fax: (202) 537-3007
e-mail: dpf@dpf.org
Web site: www.dpf.org

The foundation supports the creation of drug policies that respect individual rights, protect community health, and minimize the involvement of the criminal justice system. It opposes student drug testing and supports legalizing many drugs and increasing the number of treatment programs for addicts. Its publications include the bimonthly *Drug Policy Letter* and the book *The Great Drug War*. It also distributes *Press Clips*, an annual compilation of newspaper articles on drug legalization issues as well as legislative updates.

Drug Watch International
PO Box 45218, Omaha, NE 68145-0218
(402) 384-9212 or (505) 259-8300
Web site: www.drugwatch.org

Drug Watch International is a nonprofit drug information network that provides students, the media, and policy makers with current information from expert sources in an effort to prevent drug abuse. It promotes drug policy based on scientific research and opposes efforts to legalize drugs. It publishes the online *Drug Watch* newsletter.

Join Together
441 Stuart St., 7th Fl., Boston, MA 02116
(617) 437-1500 • fax: (617) 437-9394

e-mail: info@jointogether.org
Web site: www.jointogether.org

Founded in 1991, Join Together supports community-based efforts to reduce, prevent, and treat substance abuse. It publishes a quarterly newsletter as well as community action kits to facilitate grassroots efforts to increase awareness of substance abuse issues.

Marijuana Policy Project
PO Box 77492-Capitol Hill, Washington, DC 20013
(202) 462-5747 • fax: (202) 232-0442
e-mail: mpp@mpp.org
Web site: www.mpp.org

The Marijuana Policy Project develops and promotes policies to minimize the harm associated with marijuana. It favors legalizing the cultivation and possession of small amounts of marijuana for personal use. The project increases public awareness of the issues surrounding marijuana laws through speaking engagements, educational seminars, mass media communications, and briefing papers.

Multidisciplinary Association for Psychedelic Studies (MAPS)
2121 Commonwealth Ave., Suite 220, Charlotte, NC 28205
(941) 924-6277 • fax: (941) 924-6265
e-mail: info@maps.org
Web site: www.maps.org

MAPS is a membership-based research and educational organization. It focuses on the development of beneficial, socially sanctioned uses of psychedelic drugs and marijuana. MAPS helps scientific researchers obtain governmental approval for, fund, conduct, and report on psychedelic research involving human volunteers. It publishes the quarterly *MAPS Bulletin* as well as various reports and newsletters, such as *Dangerous Lessons: Urine Testing in Public Schools*.

Narcotic Educational Foundation of America (NEFA)
28245 Crocker Ave., Suite 230
Santa Clarita, CA 91355-1201

(661) 775-6968 • fax: (661) 775-1648
e-mail: membership@cnoa.org
Web site: www.cnoa.org/NEFA.htm

The Narcotic Educational Foundation of America was founded in 1924 to educate the public about the dangers of drug abuse. NEFA conducts research and distributes printed materials on all aspects of drug abuse. It maintains a speakers bureau and makes pamphlets and a series of Student Reference Sheets available to the public on its Web site.

National Center on Addiction and Substance Abuse at Columbia University (CASA)
633 Third Ave., 19th Floor, New York, NY 10017
(212) 841-5200 • fax: (212) 956-8020
Web site: www.casacolumbia.org

CASA is a private nonprofit organization that works to educate the public about the costs and hazards of substance abuse and the prevention and treatment of all forms of chemical dependency. The center supports treatment as the best way to reduce chemical dependency. It produces publications describing the harmful effects of alcohol and drug addiction and effective ways to address the problem of substance abuse. Several studies are available on its Web site, including *Malignant Neglect: Substance Abuse and America's Schools*.

National Clearinghouse for Alcohol and Drug Information
PO Box 2345, Rockville, MD 20847-2345
(800) 729-6686 or (301) 468-2600
fax: (301) 468-6433
e-mail: shs@health.org
Web site: www.health.org

The clearinghouse distributes publications of the U.S. Department of Health and Human Services, the National Institute on Drug Abuse, and other federal agencies concerned with alcohol and drug abuse. Free posters, kits, and pamphlets are available.

National Institute on Drug Abuse (NIDA)

U.S. Department of Health and Human Services
6001 Executive Blvd., Rm. 5213 MSC 9561
Bethesda, MD 20892-9561
(301) 443-6245
e-mail: information@lists.nida.nih.gov
Web site: www.nida.nih.gov

NIDA supports and conducts research on drug abuse—including the yearly *Monitoring the Future Survey*—to improve addiction prevention, treatment, and policy efforts. It publishes the bimonthly *NIDA Notes* newsletter, the periodic "NIDA Capsules" fact sheets, and a catalog of research reports and public education materials on drug testing and related issues.

National Organization for the Reform of Marijuana Laws (NORML)

1001 Connecticut Ave. NW, Suite 710, Washington, DC 20036
(202) 483-5500 • fax: (202) 483-0057
e-mail: natlnorml@aol.com
Web site: www.norml.org

NORML fights to legalize marijuana and to help those who have been convicted and sentenced for possessing or selling marijuana. In addition to pamphlets and position papers, it publishes the newsletter *Marijuana Highpoints*, the bimonthly *Legislative Bulletin* and *Freedom@NORML*, and the monthly *Potpourri*.

Office of National Drug Control Policy (ONDCP)

Executive Office of the President, Drugs and Crime Clearinghouse
PO Box 6000, Rockville, MD 20849-6000
e-mail: ondcp@ncjrs.org
Web site: www.whitehousedrugpolicy.gov

The Office of National Drug Control Policy is responsible for formulating the government's national drug strategy and the president's antidrug policy as well as coordinating the federal agencies responsible for stopping drug trafficking. Its Web site offers instant access to the free e-brochure *What You Need to Know About Starting a Student Drug Testing Program*.

Partnership for a Drug-Free America

405 Lexington Ave., Suite 1601, New York, NY 10174
(212) 922-1560 • fax: (212) 922-1570
Web site: www.drugfreeamerica.org

The Partnership for a Drug-Free America is a nonprofit organization that utilizes media communication to reduce demand for illicit drugs in America. It provides easy access to first person accounts, research and statistics, answers to common questions, and treatment options. It publishes the annual *Partnership Newsletter* as well as monthly press releases about current events.

Student Drug Testing Coalition

203 Main St., Suite 327, Flemington, NJ 08822
(908) 284-5080 • fax: (908) 284-5081
e-mail: drugfreesc@aol.com
Web site: www.studentdrugtesting.org

The Student Drug Testing Coalition provides students, schools, and communities the resources to implement a nonpunitive school drug-testing program. Its Web site offers links to studies, sample policies, funding options, the CD-rom *Student Drug Testing: Separating Fact from Fiction*, and the document *Student Drug-Testing Programs: Overview and Resource Guide*.

Books

Babbit, Nikki, *Adolescent Drug and Alcohol Abuse: How to Spot It, Stop It, and Get Help for Your Family.* Sebastapol, CA: O'Reilly, 2000.

Carson-DeWitt, Rosalyn, ed., *Drugs, Alcohol, and Tobacco: Learning About Addictive Behavior.* New York: Macmillan Reference USA, 2003.

Colvin, Rod, *Prescription Drug Addiction: The Hidden Epidemic.* Omaha, NE: Addicus, 2002.

Courtwright, David E., *Forces of Habit: Drugs and the Making of the Modern World.* Cambridge, MA: Harvard University Press, 2001.

Goldberg, Raymond, *Taking Sides: Drugs and Society.* Guilford, CT: McGraw-Hill/Dushkin, 2000.

Goldstein, Avram, *Addiction: From Biology to Drug Policy.* New York: Oxford University Press, 2001.

Gray, James P., *Why Our Drug Laws Have Failed and What We Can Do About It.* Philadelphia: Temple University Press, 2001.

Hyde, Margaret O., and John F. Setaro, *Drugs 101: An Overview for Teens.* Brookfield, CT: Twenty-First Century, 2003.

Jay, Jeff, and Debra Erickson Jay, *Love First: A New Approach to Intervention for Alcoholism and Drug Addiction.* Minneapolis: Hazelden, 2000.

Ketcham, Katherine, and Nicolas A. Pace, *Teens Under the Influence.* New York: Ballantine, 2003.

Maran, Meredith, *Dirty: A Search for Awareness Inside America's Teenage Drug Epidemic.* San Francisco: HarperSanFrancisco, 2003.

Meier, Barry, *Pain Killer: A "Wonder" Drug's Trail of Addiction and Death*. Emmaus, PA: Rodale, 2003.

Mogil, Cindy R., *Swallowing a Bitter Pill*. Far Hills, NJ: New Horizon, 2001.

Roleff, Tamera L., ed., *Drug Abuse*. San Diego: Greenhaven, 2005.

Shapiro, Susan, *Lighting Up: How I Stopped Smoking, Drinking, and Everything Else I Loved in Life Except Sex*. New York: Bantam Deli, 2005.

Periodicals

Alcoholism & Drug Abuse Weekly, "Survey: One-in-Five Teens Abuse Prescription Drugs," May 2, 2005.

Bogard, Kimber L., "Affluent Adolescents, Depression, and Drug Use: The Role of Adults in Their Lives," *Adolescence*, Summer 2005.

Bosse, Ben, "Designing Effective Youth Prevention Programming," *Addiction Professional*, March 2005.

Brunk, Doug, "Report Documents Magnitude of U.S. Substance Abuse: Data Show Children Face Multiple Risks," *Clinical Psychiatry News*, May 2005.

Campus Crime, "Scientists Determine Most Effective Ways to Deter College Drug Use," June 2004.

Checca, Carey, "No Tolerance Story," *Newark (NJ) Advocate*, August 1, 2003.

Diego, Miguel A., Tiffany M. Field, and Christopher E. Sanders, "Academic Performance, Popularity, and Depression Predict Adolescent Substance Abuse," *Adolescence*, Spring 2003.

Emerling, Gary, "Students Advocate Random Drug Tests," *Washington Times*, June 12, 2005.

Fay, Calvina L., "Student Drug Testing Is Part of the Solution," *Behavioral Health Management*, July/August 2004.

Gordon, Andrea, "Expert Urges Using Common Sense with Teens," *Toronto Star*, July 18, 2005.

Gordon, Susan B., "Teen Drug Abuse: Underlying Pyschological Disorders and Parental Attitudes Have a Big Effect on Teens' Addictive Behavior," *Behavioral Health Management,* September/October 2003.

Jancin, Bruce, "Substance Abuse Trajectory Begins in Early Childhood," *Pediatric News,* July 2005.

Koch Kubetin, Sally, "Screen for Drug Use Risk with Two Questions: School Failure, Lack of Close Adults," *Pediatric News,* November 2003.

Little, Linda, "Strive for Confidentiality in Talks About Drugs," *Clinical Psychiatry News,* June 2005.

Miller, Sara B., "Steps Toward More Drug Testing in School," *Christian Science Monitor,* May 20, 2005.

Modern Brewery Age, "CASA Survey Says Boredom to Blame for Teen Substance Abuse," August 25, 2003.

Riccio, Nina, "To Test or Not to Test?" *Current Health 2,* March 2003.

Rosenbaum, Marsha, "Random Student Drug Testing Is No Panacea," *Alcoholism & Drug Abuse Weekly,* April 12, 2004.

Saunders, Debra J., "Student Drug Testing Is Un-American," *San Francisco Chronicle,* April 17, 2005.

Science World, "Two Teen Health Dangers: Obesity & Drug Addiction," May 9, 2005.

Smith, Larry, "Prescription Drugs: More Teens Are Popping Pills for an Easy High," *Teen People,* May 1, 2003.

Stoil, Michael J., "Teen Drug Use's Changing Profile: The Bush Administration Claims a Victory in Reducing Teen Drug Abuse, but the Data Also Show Some Disturbing Trends," *Behavioral Health Management,* May/June 2005.

Wagner, Arlo, "Schools Reject Drug Testing Policy," *Washington Times,* August 19, 2004.

Wittberger, Pat, "Jenny's Journey," *Ashore,* Winter 2003.

Web Sites

KidsHealth (www.kidshealth.org). KidsHealth is one of the largest sites on the Internet providing doctor-approved health information about children from before birth through adolescence. The Web site provides teens with information on drugs, addiction, and treatment.

Phoenix House (www.phoenixhouse.org). Founded in 1967, the Phoenix House is the largest nonprofit drug and alcohol treatment organization in the United States. Its Web site provides referrals to drug abuse treatment facilities and offers education and prevention resources on drug abuse.

Substance Abuse Treatment Facility Locator (www.findtreatment.samhsa.gov). This Web site is sponsored by the Substance Abuse and Mental Health Services Administration (SAMHSA). It includes over ten thousand treatment programs for adults and teens.

Hotlines

National Drug Information Treatment and Referral Hotline
(800) 662-HELP (4357)

Substance Abuse 24-Hour Helpline and Treatment
(800) 234-0420

Youth Crisis Hotline
(800) 448-4663

drug testing is barrier to, 48,
62–63
Supreme Court decision
allows drug testing in, 59,
69–70

Fourth Amendment, 56, 68,
69

Gelender, Amanda, 78
Gunja, Fatema, 42
Guymon Public Schools
(Oklahoma), 60

hair test, 19, 21
masking agents for, 87–88
health education, 99–100
Hunterdon Central Regional
High School (New Jersey),
51, 57

In re F.B. (1999), 70, 74

Johnson, Lloyd D., 43
Jordan, Kathy, 107
Journal of School Health, 43
Joye v. Hunterdon Central
Regional High School Board of
Education (2003), 72

Kelley-Fritz, Audrey, 33–35

law enforcement, 26, 105–106

marijuana, 19, 43
Monitoring the Future (survey),
43–44

National Drug Control
Strategy, 27
National Survey of American
Attitudes on Substance
Abuse, 7
Nelson, Roman, 102

Office of Personnel
Management (OPM), 14
Orchard, Annie, 107

parents, 24, 95
can prevent teen substance
abuse, 26, 29, 41
oppose student drug testing,
45–46
Partnership for a Drug-Free
America, 103
peer pressure, 44, 107
drug use and, 25–26
Polk County (Florida), 33–35
Pollock, Tamara, 81
prescription drugs, abuse of,
25
Presslak, Rudy, 32
Prince, Helen, 104–105
Project Northland
(Minnesota), 98
Project STAR/Midwestern
Prevention Project, 100
Provet, Peter, 9–10

Reagan, Ronald, 14, 84
Rorvig, Leah B., 37
Rosenbaum, Marsha, 42, 78

saliva test, 21, 52, 88

Schmidt, Joseph G., 31, 32
school "connectedness," 89, 90, 93–94
schools, 22–24
  drug testing in, 38–39, 43, 57–59
  safety in, 95–97
Simon, Ray, 107
social and emotional learning (SEL), 97
St. Patrick High School (Chicago), 31–33
Stockton, Neal, 103–104, 108
substance abuse, 10, 29, 72
  prevalence of, among teens, 7, 25–26
  prevention of, 45, 107
    police involvement in, 105–106
    role of parents in, 26, 29, 30
    school "connectedness" and, 90–94
sweat test, 19, 21

teachers, 45, 94
Tecumseh, Oklahoma BOE v. Earls (2002), 59, 64, 69
Theodore, Jennifer, 67
Theodore, Kimberly, 67
Theodore v. Delaware Valley School District v. Earls (2003), 64, 67, 70
  ruling in, 68, 73–76
Todd v. Rush County Schools (1998), 56

urine test, 19, 20
  masking agents for, 87–88

Veronia School District v. Acton (1995), 55, 64, 68

Walters, John, 40, 107
White House Office of National Drug Control Policy (ONDCP), 27
Williams v. Secretary of Navy (1986), 14–15
Wolfe, Adam T., 64

ABOUT THE EDITOR

Patty Jo Sawvel, a freelance journalist and graduate of the Wake Forrest University Addiction Studies Program for Journalists, has specialized in student drug abuse research for over a decade. She received a first place award from the North Carolina Press Association for investigative reporting on "Drugs in Schools," which is a basis for her current book project. She contributed chapters to *Drugs and Controlled Substances: Information for Students*, authored numerous regional publications, and is a biweekly columnist for the *High Point Enterprise* and the *Kernersville News* in North Carolina. She and her husband, Don, have three children.